RILKE'S LATE POETRY

ALSO BY GRAHAM GOOD

The Observing Self: Rediscovering the Essay
(London and New York: Routledge, 1988)

*Humanism Betrayed: Theory, Ideology and Culture
in the Contemporary University*
(Kingston and Montreal: McGill-Queen's
University Press, 2001)

Rilke's Late Poetry

Duino Elegies
The Sonnets to Orpheus
Selected Last Poems

Translated with an Introduction
& Commentary by

GRAHAM GOOD

RONSDALE PRESS

RILKE'S LATE POETRY: DUINO ELEGIES,
THE SONNETS TO ORPHEUS, AND SELECTED LAST POEMS.
Translations, Introduction and Commentary © 2004 by Graham Good
Third Printing May 2011

RONSDALE PRESS
3350 West 21st Avenue
Vancouver, B.C., Canada V6S 1G7
www.ronsdalepress.com

Typesetting: Julie Cochrane, in New Baskerville 11 pt on 13.5
Cover Design: Julie Cochrane
Cover Art: Satoshi Nagasaka, based on an image of the 1915 bust of Rilke by the
     Swiss sculptor Fritz Huf.
Printing: Island Blue, Victoria, B.C., Canada

Ronsdale Press wishes to thank the following for their support of its publishing program: the Canada Council for the Arts, the Government of Canada through the Canada Book Fund, and the Province of British Columbia through the Book Publishing Tax Credit Program and the British Columbia Arts Council.

Library and Archives Canada Cataloguing in Publication

Rilke, Rainer Maria, 1875–1926.
   Rilke's late poetry: Duino elegies, the sonnets to Orpheus and
selected last poems / Rainer Maria Rilke; translated by Graham Good.

Translated from the German.
ISBN 1-55380-024-9

   1. Rilke, Rainer Maria, 1875-1926 — Criticism and interpretation.
I. Good, Graham II. Title.

PT2635.I65A24 2005   831'.912   C2005-900259-X

For Pamela Nagasaka

CONTENTS

ACKNOWLEDGEMENTS

I would like to acknowledge help with these translations from Dr. Robert Fagles and Dr. Ralph Freedman, who supervised my PhD dissertation at Princeton University; the late Dr Peter Loeffler of the University of British Columbia; Peter Haworth, who organized dramatic readings of some of the poems; Elise Partridge, who gave helpful and encouraging comments; and Dr. Marketa Goetz-Stankiewicz, Dr. Markus Hallensleben, and Dr. Petra Ganzenmuller, all of the University of British Columbia, who read portions of the text and made valuable suggestions.

INTRODUCTION

– I. A Tale of Two Castles:
 The Composition of the Late Poetry

The late poetry of Rainer Maria Rilke (1875–1926) is one of the sum-mits of European poetry in the twentieth century. As an inquiry into, and expression of, the human condition in the modern era, it has lost none of its relevance, and probably gained more.

The late poetry consists of the work Rilke completed between early 1922 and his death in late 1926. *Duino Elegies,* a set of ten long philo-sophical meditations, were in fact begun in 1912 and worked on in-termittently over ten years, but more than half of the work belongs to February 1922. Besides this miraculous breakthrough, the same month also saw the unexpected birth and completion of a new work, *The Sonnets to Orpheus,* in two parts consisting together of 55 sonnets. The third part of the late poetry consists of the mostly short lyrics Rilke wrote in the following five years up to his death in December 1926.

The first of the two castles associated with the late poetry is Duino Castle, a huge structure occupying a promontory on the Adriatic Sea near Trieste, then part of the Austro-Hungarian Empire. The castle was on the front line of hostilities when Italy entered the Great War in 1915, and was irreparably damaged by bombardment from the Italian navy. It was the property of Rilke's aristocratic patron Princess Marie von Thurn und Taxis-Hohenlohe. She and her husband also owned a palace in Venice, and a castle in what is now the Czech Republic. Rilke spent the winter of 1911–1912 in Duino castle, most-ly alone. He was driven down by a chauffeur from Paris in the Princess's car, a trip which lasted nine days.

Rilke described his situation at Duino in a letter to Hedwig Fischer of 25 October 1911: "This castle, immensely towering above the sea . . . looks out with many of its windows (one of mine included) into the most open sea-space, directly into the universe, you might say, and into its generous, all-surpassing spectacles." Two months later, though, he was feeling more confined than liberated by this unique setting. He confided to Lou Andreas-Salomé on 28 December: "This year I am enjoying the hospitality of friends here (for the time being all alone) in this strong old castle that holds one a little like a prisoner: it cannot do otherwise with its immense walls."

One stormy evening he was out on the battlements when he seemed to hear a voice in the wind declaiming what became the opening lines of *The First Elegy*. Rilke also began several other *Elegies* at Duino: the *Second, Third, Sixth, Ninth* and *Tenth*, but only the *First* and *Second* were completed there. In 1913 he managed to complete the *Third* and add to the *Sixth*, and in 1915 wrote the whole of the *Fourth*. The Great War and its immediate aftermath seemed to destroy not only the aristocratic, cosmopolitan Europe that was his milieu, but also his poetic inspiration. It did not return until early 1922. Rilke was left stateless by the break-up of the Austro-Hungarian empire, though he eventually acquired a Czech passport through his birth and upbringing in Prague. He was also homeless, as his apartment in Paris had been taken over by the authorities and his property seized.

Finally, after a long search, and with the help of another wealthy patron, he found a modest castle of his own in Muzot (pronounced "Muzotte," according to Rilke), a village in the French-speaking Valais region of Switzerland. He described it as a typical medieval *manoir,* consisting "only of one strong house-body . . . that included everything," a shape that fitted him "like a suit of armour." The image of containment echoes his description of Duino, as does the open outlook, "with views into the valley, over to the mountain slopes and into the most wonderful depths of sky" (letter to Princess Marie von Thurn und Taxis-Hohenlohe, 25 July 1921).

It was from here that Rilke wrote to Princess Marie on 11 February 1922 to announce the completion of all ten *Elegies* and the unexpected arrival of *The Sonnets to Orpheus:* "Miracle. Grace. — All in a few days. It was a hurricane, as at Duino that time: all that was fibre, fabric in me, cracked and bent. Eating was not to be thought of . . . I went out and stroked, as if it were a great old beast, the little Muzot that had sheltered all this for me, that had, at last, *vouchsafed* it to me." W.H. Auden described this moment in 1938 in the nineteenth of his *Sonnets from China:*

Tonight in China let me think of one
Who for ten years of drought and silence waited,
Until in Muzot all his being spoke,
And everything was given once for all.
Awed, grateful, tired, content to die, completed,
He went out in the winter night to stroke
That tower as one strokes an animal.

― *II. The Spiritual Crisis of Modernity:* Duino Elegies

Rilke's ten long philosophical poems are called "elegies" for two reasons, the first connected with their form, and the second with their content. Formally, except for the *Fourth* and *Eighth,* they use an "elegiac metre," that is a dactylic metre (a dactyl being a stressed syllable followed by two unstressed ones) which is a loose variant of the elegiac distich (a pair of lines consisting of a dactylic hexameter and a dactylic pentameter). Rilke's lines are highly irregular in length and metre, but have a perceptible dactylic base. This combination of flexibility and continuity is perfectly adapted to the exploratory nature of the poems. The *Elegies* do not present achieved solutions, but rather invite the reader to participate in a discovery process which contains more questions than answers. The driving rhythm constantly renews the quest for meanings, producing within each poem a series of attempts at understanding which often end in bafflement or failure, but are immediately followed by a fresh attempt, using different voices (the poem has some of the polyphonic elements of T.S. Eliot's *The Waste Land,* also first published in 1922, which was originally entitled "He do the police in different voices"). The tentative, unsettled quality of the verse produces a sequence of possible approximations, and provisional insights rather than established certainties.

In terms of content, *Duino Elegies* belong to the German elegy tradition practised by Goethe, Schiller, Hölderlin and others. Here, the theme is not so much the lament for a dead person as a meditation on general issues of life-experience, spirituality and culture. In Rilke's case the central issue is the spiritual crisis of modernity. The general view presented by the poet sees modern culture as having lost the spiritual dimension of life. We are no longer in touch with gods or angels, and they have become terrifying to us. At the same time, with the replacement of traditional art and craft by mass-produced consumer goods we have lost much of the concrete texture of existence as well, lost the reassurance of having long-lasting traditional artifacts ("things" in the full sense) as part of our lives.

In Rilke's view, the combination of these two losses (of spirituality and of physicality) has made our experience shallow and superficial. Our buildings are inhuman, abstract structures, and our art mostly fails to contain and preserve our self-expression, as it did in earlier epochs, notably Classical Greece. We've become both spectators, watching the world and ourselves from a detached viewpoint, and performers, assuming and dropping roles which always fail to represent our inner feelings. Even a puppet show or a group of vagrant acrobats would be more authentic than the pretences we put on for each other in our family or society.

Modernity, for Rilke, resembles a huge nightmarish fun-fair, full of cheap distractions and false promises which we use to hide from authentic emotion and experience, especially the experience of grief. Grief and death are shunned and denied, yet paradoxically this creates great fear of them. We are dominated by the fear of loss, and clutch possessions and people all the more anxiously out of insecurity. We see the world in terms of fear for ourselves, fear for our future, fear of our individual destiny. This separates us from reality, so that we cannot see things as themselves. We are always *opposite* the world, never fully *in* it.

The poet contrasts this typically modern state of mind with other forms of consciousness, human and non-human. Angels (Rilke was concerned that his understanding of these beings as impersonal spiritual intensities roaming the cosmos should not be confused with the Christian conception) know that life and death constitute a single undivided realm, a double kingdom; unlike humans, who try to remain within the life portion, the angels inhabit both. Lovers sometimes catch a glimpse of spiritual intensity, but cannot fully open to it because they are usually too concerned with keeping each other; abandoned lovers are actually more able to experience this intensity through their grief. Heroes are those who aim directly for self-realization, choosing and controlling their destiny without fear of death. Children, until adults push them into growing up, accept death as something inward, not something dreadfully lurking in the future. Animals, without awareness of a separate identity, are unself-consciously *in* the world, not mere spectators of it. They do not dread death, even if at times they feel nostalgia for the security of the womb. All of these forms of consciousness, neglected or suppressed in the modern world, hold powerful lessons for us if we pay attention to them.

Is there a way out of the modern predicament? The poet eventually arrives at certain possibilities. We can cherish the monuments and artifacts that remain to us from the past, the heritage of human culture. We can nurture our awareness of the dead, listen to their voices, and show humility and reverence towards these past existences. Most of all, we can diminish our self-preoccupation, our obsession with our personal identity, image, and performance, and accept the task that Nature has assigned us.

What is this task? Rilke reverses the common idea that we humans need Nature, and asserts that Nature needs us. Nature is seeking to perfect itself through human consciousness — only this can completely fulfill the natural world. Nature needs us to reflect her beauty back to herself, amplified by our delight. This delight, once embodied in more lasting artifacts, can now best be expressed in acceptance of transience. Transience should not be rejected, but celebrated and even intensified. Our task is no longer to preserve and contain, but enjoy and praise; to turn the visible into the invisible, and transpose the transient outer world into the even more transient dimension of consciousness.

The poet concludes that the solution to the spiritual crisis of modernity is not so much poetry, art and culture as such, but their use as the means to a higher, purer, more inward, more spiritual awareness, which is no longer so dependent on outer objectification.

The poet combines a lament for the passing of authentic "things," whether classed as handicraft or as artwork, with a finally optimistic sense of human destiny moving beyond the concrete and visible, into a more spiritual consciousness.

– *III. Living Poetically:* The Sonnets to Orpheus

Just as Rilke radicalized the traditional elegy form in *Duino Elegies,* he radicalized the sonnet form in *The Sonnets to Orpheus.* Certainly he maintained the fourteen lines and full rhyme scheme in all fifty-five poems, though some rhyme schemes are irregular. But metre and line-length are subjected to great variations. Some sonnets have long dactylic lines, reminiscent of the *Elegies,* which run up to fifteen or sixteen syllables, while others are pared down to two or three words. Furthermore, line-lengths can vary considerably within the same poem. Gone is the tidy containment of the traditional sonnet; a sense of irrepressible excitement seems constantly to push the edges of the form while always preserving the unifying force of rhyme.

The Sonnets are inscribed "as a memorial for Wera Ouckama Knoop," the daughter of a friend of Rilke's, who died in 1919 at the age of nineteen. Wera (pronounced Vera) appears in only a few of the sonnets, mostly near the beginning and ending of each cycle, and is usually seen as a dancer. She represents the theme of early death, already explored in the *Elegies.* In this aspect, *The Sonnets'* theme is closer to the normal English understanding of "elegy" as a lament for a dead person than is that of the *Elegies* themselves.

The second key figure is Orpheus, whose familiarity with Death's kingdom links him with Wera. The first cycle begins with Orpheus charming all the animals into silence with his lyre (a scene Rilke knew from an Italian Renaissance engraving by Giovanni Battista Cima da Conegliano), and ends with his dismemberment by the Maenads, the demented female followers of Dionysus. Although explicit scenes from the myth are few, Orpheus is invoked throughout, often directly addressed as "you." His spirit pervades not only the sphere of poetry, music and song symbolized by the lyre, but also represents creativity in general, in Nature and culture alike. The creativity of human civilization may be expressed in fountains, vases, tombs, towers and cities. It may even include modern technological inventions, though the machine represents a danger to humanity if it dominates rather than serves. At times Orpheus is also associated with the creativity of Nature, expressed in fruit, flowers, blossoms, trees, branches, roots and the seasons. Among the most powerful symbols of creativity are those which combine the human and the natural: water flowing through fountains, the dead nourishing the earth, or the willow bough bending into a lyre. Almost every sonnet finds a fresh occasion for celebrating creative renewal.

Despite this insistence on celebration (and ultimately because of it), the death theme is never far away. Just as in *The Tenth Elegy* grief leads us to the wellsprings of joy, so in *The Sonnets* the acceptance of death and sorrow creates a space for their transformation into affirmative forces. Denying death and clinging to life leads to rigidity and fear of change, which ultimately make us more vulnerable to destruction. Transformation can only take place if we are willing to abandon present forms, habits and structures in the faith that we will find new ones. This means accepting loss, accepting transience in ourselves and everything around us, as the prelude to rediscovery. Suffering and misery are woven into the fabric of existence, and are a vital part of "the whole glorious design."

Poetry is not seen as a triumph over transience, but as a celebration of it. Where Shakespeare's sonnets proclaim the immortalization of his love in rhyme that will outlast monuments, Rilke's sonnets rejoice in their own temporary, provisional quality. Decay is not something to mourn or resist. Poetry is not a separate enclosure, walled off from time and decay: poetry is existence. Song is being, conceived broadly enough to encompass non-being as well. It is a heightening of ordinary life-processes, like breathing, which one sonnet describes as an "invisible poem." Poetry is breath, breeze, wind, not monument. It accepts inspiration (breathing in) and expiration (breathing out) as belonging together. In another image, the poet describes Orpheus' heart as a "transient press" which paradoxically produces a permanent supply of wine.

The figure of the poet, who is the speaker of the sonnets and the voice which invokes Orpheus, is not finally distinct either from humanity in general (the "we" of the *Elegies* recurs here) or from Orpheus himself. The poet is a transitional figure whose identity shades into that of Orpheus in one direction, as well as into that of the ordinary human such as the reader in the other. Orpheus represents in heightened form a consciousness which is accessible to us all, and is even natural to us, though overlaid in the modern period by technological distractions and materialism.

The god, the poet, and eventually the reader combine into a unified field where images and symbols, feelings and ideas, can appear and disappear freely, unimpeded by clinging and possessiveness. Disappearing is as important as breathing out; each is the essential prelude to the next appearance or inbreath. The poems model this fluency in the way the cycles are organized, so that one poem flows into another, recycling the key words and themes. For example, the theme of breath opens and closes the second cycle, but also occurs intermittently throughout: breath, or similar ideas, like wind or breeze, often end a poem (see Part I, sonnet 3, 4 and 8, for example) and form an easy transition to the next. Breath enables sound to emerge from humans as song.

Poetry is identified with breath, but also with sound. The nature of sound is to arise and die away. That is why it is a better symbol of Rilke's Orphic conception of poetry (and of life) than symbols based on sight, where the temporary quality is often less evident. Sound cannot last: it radiates outwards concentrically as it dies. The two cycles of *The Sonnets* are circular, radiating outwards from the thematic centre provided by Orpheus and Wera. The second cycle, slightly longer, could be seen as enclosing the first with variations and echoes. The circle image also extends to listening. Sound, as its vibrations spread outwards, creates circles of listeners, temporary communities of hearers, like the animals who gather round, forgetting their own strident cries, as in Part I, sonnet 1.

The voice at the centre of the poems often resembles that of a shaman or mage. Many sonnets begin with a naming which is also a summoning up of the being who is named. Rose, fountain, flower and many others are saluted in the opening words; they are explicitly addressed as "you" and called up. Human addressees include judges, childhood playmates, the dancer. Sometimes the "you" is Orpheus. After the initial summons, those addressed are celebrated but also commanded. The poems are full of exhortations: "Will transformation." "Dance the orange." Many statements have a certainty and authority that is absent from the *Elegies*, but can emerge after their uncertainties. "Song is being." "The earth gives." The voice has a vatic quality, as if the poet has taken on aspects of the god he summons, Orpheus. His voice becomes "one of Nature's mouths." The poet moves beyond self, beyond the merely personal, and lets his words be a vehicle for a wider wisdom to move through.

Orpheus also becomes a symbol of transformation. Besides raising the lyre among the dead, he continued to sing after the Maenads tore his head off and floated it down the river. Orpheus can move back and forth between the two kingdoms of life and death, and is thus identified with the capacity to transform. Transformation is not a way of evading death, but accepting it as prelude to finding a new form. Dismembered, a "scattered god," Orpheus lives and dies in every moment of beauty, and its celebration in song. "Once and for all, it's Orpheus when there's singing." Song itself is a form of transformation, not preservation. He goes *through* "the narrow lyre." He is not an aesthete or a formalist who sees the poem as a beautiful object. Rather, art is a means of transcendence. "The lyre's trellis doesn't tie his hand." As voice, the poem summons up and then surrenders both its content and itself to further transformations, in the reader and in the world. Music, like poetry, has structure, and builds a "deified house," but only with the "most vibrating stones."

Poetry is praise and affirmation. Praise is the "task," an important term for Rilke, equivalent to "vocation." Poetic awareness is the "task" assigned to us by nature. Poetry is a calling. The poet is summoned himself as well as summoning other beings. Orpheus is explicitly "summoned to praise." Praise even encompasses grief, for grief can fully express itself only in the "precincts" of praise. Only the singer knows "the losses of the earth," precisely because he *nevertheless* praises the heart which endures them.

– IV. The Last Poems

In the five last years of his life, Rilke wrote a number of mostly short poems, often as occasional pieces or dedications. These "Last Poems," as I am calling them, have not been as thoroughly explored or widely translated as the *Elegies* and *Sonnets*. Yet they seem to me to constitute a kind of Third Testament, equal in scope and intensity to the other two works. These short poems often seem to distill effortlessly the hard-won insights of the major cycles which preceded them. Some are directed to named individual recipients, and a tone of intimate familiar address is common. Some allude too closely to particular circumstances to be immediately accessible, but many offer brief luminous glimpses into the achieved serenity of the poet in these years. They have an effortless simplicity and certainty, far from the protracted struggles for understanding explored in the *Elegies*.

One pervasive theme is gratitude to Nature, first as a source of beauty, but also as a fount of wisdom. The upwelling of springs, the renewal that lurks in roots, the cycle of the seasons are all praised as inspirations for us to see our own lives as creative adventure. Death and loss are accepted completely as creating space for regeneration. Nothing is truly lost in Rilke's final world-view. "Even our losses are ours." What appears to be lost is soon recycled in a new form. Because "nothing belongs to us," we belong to everything. "What we have lost still circulates," and will come back to us, transformed. True possession is paradoxically complete surrender. The poet is someone who surrenders the word to the All: "The Word was given to him/ to lose it without a trace."

In these last poems Rilke explores the idea of the universe as a totality to which nothing can be added and from which nothing can be subtracted. Even destruction makes room for new creation: what has supposedly been eliminated returns in a new form. The All is a kind of "great relatedness" governed by laws of reciprocity, compensation, and complementarity. It replies to us if we are open enough to listen. "Our sign is answered by a counter-sign." Our silence draws an answer. We lose one thing and gain another. What we give away is given back. Just as a particular sight is lost to view, we can "recollect it in a nearby face," where a human expression records a response to what has vanished.

The poems often demonstrate this effect of counterweight or counterpressure by showing a human feeling or perception being absorbed and returned by the world. "What we cannot grasp, grasps us." We complete Nature, and Nature completes us. Poetry is an art of surrender, or receptivity. Self-fulfillment comes through a kind of emptying of the self or loss of self. If we leave a space, something will come to fill it. As regards the risks we run through exposure to Nature, "we are ultimately sheltered by / our very unprotectedness." There is a continuous interchange between self and world, changing places, each becoming the other. True inwardness is identified as "intensified sky," a heightened version of the outside world.

Rilke died of leukemia on 29 December 1926, and was buried in Raron, Switzerland, on 2 January 1927. His grave bore the epitaph he had composed about a year before:

Rose: oh pure contradiction, desire to be
no one's sleep beneath so many
eyelids.

– V. The Translations

The translations are based on the texts of the most recent standard edition: Rainer Maria Rilke, *Werke: Kommentierte Ausgabe in vier Bänden*, edited by Manfred Engel, Ulrich Fülleborn, Horst Nalewski and August Stahl (Frankfurt a.M.: Insel Verlag, 1996). The translated texts are all contained in Volume 2, edited by Manfred Engel and Ulrich Fülleborn. I have reproduced the section breaks and indentations in *Duino Elegies* as they appear in that text; there is some variation in the German editions of Rilke.

My aim as a translator has been to give a rendering that reads effectively in the basic idiom of contemporary English poetry, while reproducing as many as possible of the formal features of the originals. In the *Elegies* this means preserving the lineation for most of the time, as well as the driving dactylic metre that gives the work its characteristic energy. In *The Sonnets* it means keeping the rhyme scheme as far as possible without distorting the sense. Rilke always uses a full rhyme scheme, but I have had to admit half-rhymes (a common practice in modern English verse) and occasionally omit rhymes altogether. The wide variety of line lengths and metres is also preserved. The Last Poems may be rhymed or unrhymed in the original, and I have allowed myself more latitude here in giving mostly unrhymed translations of rhymed originals, since these poems are not a formal unified cycle like *The Sonnets to Orpheus*.

Translation means a crossing of temporal as well as linguistic boundaries. As well as being transferred from German to English, Rilke's poetry now has to be transferred from the early twentieth to the early twenty-first century. 1922 was the year of *The Waste Land* as well as the *Elegies* and *Sonnets,* and after T.S. Eliot's poem certain expressions became unusable in English poetry. The diction of German poetry was not modernized so drastically as English poetry was by T.S. Eliot and Ezra Pound. Instead, a more gradual process of modernization took place, which was not really complete until, say, the advent of Brecht, a generation younger than Rilke. The poetic idiom even of Rilke's late poetry includes some elements which would sound archaic to modern readers of poetry in English: thus I have omitted exclamations such as "Woe!" or "Alas!"

Translation is also interpretation, as the variety of versions of Rilke in English testify. The density and complexity of his poetic thought means that many possibilities of interpretation are latent in the German, forcing a decision by the translator of which meaning or shade of meaning to use. When the exigencies of rhyme and metre are added to the task of phrasing the meaning, a tight web of interacting constraints is created, within which the translator has to work. The poems become travellers in space and time, with all the risks, losses, and excitements that entails. Poems that speak constantly of transformation themselves undergo transformation as they move through different readings, different historical periods and different languages. I hope that the present versions may play a part in this process.

DUINO ELEGIES

The First Elegy

If I cried aloud, would anyone hear me among the ranks
of the angels? And even if one of them suddenly
took me to heart, I'd be overwhelmed by his
more powerful being. For beauty is simply
the onset of terror, which we're hardly able to bear,
and can only admire because it so coolly neglects
to destroy us. Angels are terrifying.
    And so I restrain myself, and choke back
the dark sobs, the appeal for help. For who
can help us? Not angels, not humans,
and the knowing animals have noticed already
how uneasy we are in our interpreted world.
All we have left is perhaps a certain tree on a slope
to look at day after day; or yesterday's streets,
or a steadfastly loyal old habit, which liked it with us,
and just stayed put and never went home.
    And the Night — when the wind full of world-space
eats at our faces — waits for us all,
longed-for Night with her soft disappointment
wearily facing the lonely heart. Is she kinder to lovers?
But they only use each other to hide from their Fate.
You still haven't grasped it? Throw the emptiness
out of your arms and into the spaces we breathe:
so perhaps the birds will feel their flight
more inwardly through the intensified space.

Yes, Spring needed you every time. Many stars
asked your awareness. And once in the past
a wave came rising towards you,
and once as you walked by an open window
a violin proffered itself. They set you a task.
But did you perform it? Or were you instead
still full of expectancy, as if all these things

presaged a lover for *you?* (Where could you hide her,
with your big, strange ideas so freely wandering
in and out, and often staying the night?)
But if you long to, sing about *other* lovers; their famous
passions are still in need of immortalizing.
You almost envy abandoned lovers, and find them
so much more loving than satisfied ones. Begin it
again and again, the unattainable praise.
And think about this: the Hero survives, and even defeat
is only a pretext for *being:* his latest incarnation.
But lovers are reabsorbed by exhausted Nature,
as if she lacked strength to bear them twice.
Have you thought enough about Gaspara Stampa,
so that any woman whose lover has left her
might feel: "I could be like her."
Shouldn't these age-old heartaches finally grow
more fruitful for us? Isn't it time we lovingly
freed ourselves from our lovers, and, trembling, endured,
as the arrow endures the bowstring, braced to be shot,
to be *more* than itself? For staying is nowhere.

Voices, voices. Listen, my heart, as only saints
have listened before, so the mighty answer
lifted them clean off the ground, still kneeling —
incredibly, they didn't notice, so deep was
their listening. Not that you would be able to bear it,
the voice of God, not by a long way. But listen to the wind,
the uninterrupted news developing out of the silence.
News of those who died young is reaching towards you.
Whenever you entered churches in Rome or Naples,
didn't their Fate address you quietly?
Or a noble epitaph struck you, like the plaque
you recently saw in Santa Maria Formosa.
What do they want from me? That I should gently
correct the apparent injustice that sometimes
hinders a little their spirits' movement.

Yes, it's strange, no longer living on earth,
abandoning habits you've hardly got used to,
like interpreting roses or other especially
promising objects in terms of a human future;
strange, giving up your former existence
in endlessly anxious hands, and discarding
even your own name like a broken toy.
Strange, to wish your wishes no further. Strange,
to see what was once connected cut loose
and scattered in space. It isn't easy, being dead:
you have to do a lot of retracing before you catch
a hint of eternity. They all make the same mistake,
the living, of drawing too sharp distinctions.
It's said that the angels are often unconscious
of whether they're moving among the living
or the dead. The everlasting current
flows through both kingdoms, all ages,
always the same, the dominant note in both.

Eventually those who left early no longer need us,
gently weaned from the earth, like infants
weaned from their mothers' soft breasts. But we,
in whom progress often springs from grief
(could we exist without it?), need greater secrets.
This is the point of the myth about Linos:
music began when it first dared to break
the arid, paralysed silence of mourning;
in the startled space that a god-like youth
suddenly left for ever, the void first felt
the vibrations that even now provide us
with rapture and comfort and help.

The Second Elegy

Every angel is terrifying. Yet I'll call you regardless,
you almost lethal birds of the soul,
knowing your nature. The days of Tobias are over,
when one of the brightest angels arrived on his humble doorstep,
a little disguised for travel, but hardly terror-provoking —
one youth seeing another as he looked up, curious.
But now, if the dreaded archangel took one step
in our direction from behind the stars,
our pounding hearts would kill us. Who are you?

Blessed from birth, world's favourites,
towering peaks, dawn-reddened ridges
of all creation, pollen of blossoming godhead,
junctions of light, avenues, stairways, thrones,
spaces of being, shields of joy, tumults
of wildly passionate feeling, and suddenly, alone:
Mirror! whose face reabsorbs its outflow of beauty.

But we lose ourselves through our feelings;
we breathe ourselves out and away. From ember to ember,
we give off a weaker smell. Just as someone might tell us.
"Yes, you're in my blood; this room, the Spring,
is full of you . . ." It's pointless; he cannot retain us,
we disappear within and around him. You cannot hold on to
those who are beautiful. Appearances constantly
rise in their faces and vanish. Like dew from the morning grass,
what is ours evaporates, like the warmth of a
hot dish. Smiles: where do they go to? Glances, also —
fresh, warm, transient waves from the heart . . .
and yet we *are* them. The world-space in which we dissolve,
does it taste of us afterwards? Do the angels really
only take back what has flowed from themselves,
or is there, inadvertently, sometimes a little

of our existence as well? Are we
blended into their features, like the vagueness
in pregnant women's faces? It passes unnoticed
amidst the angels' whirling return to themselves.
(And why *should* they notice it?)

Lovers, in the night air, could find a miraculous language
if they knew how to. For everything seems
to obscure us. Look: the trees *exist*. The houses
we live in still stand. We alone
pass everything by like a changing breeze.
And it all conspires to keep us secret, half
out of shame, perhaps, and half from unspeakable hope.

Lovers, so satisfied with each other,
what about *us?* You touch. But what does that prove?
Look, my hands might happen to hold
each other, or let my usual face
take refuge behind them. This gives me a small
feeling. But who would presume to *exist* on this?
But you, who passionately reach for each other
until you withdraw, overwhelmed —
no more! — you, who under each other's hands
grow riper than vintage grapes,
you, who sometimes vanish, but only because the other
has got out of hand: what about *us?* I know
you like touching because the kisses *preserve,*
because the place you lovingly cover
does not disappear; because underneath it you sense
pure permanence. Your embrace seems to promise
eternity. And yet when you withstood the shock
of the first glances, the desire at the window,
the first walk together, *once,* through the garden:
lovers, do you still *exist* as you did then? When you lift
your mouths to each other and touch, drink to drink,
the action strangely escapes from the drinker.

On the Greek stelae, weren't you amazed at how restrained
the human gestures were? Love and absence —
didn't they sit on people's shoulders more lightly, as if they
were made of different stuff than we are? Think of the hands,
how they met without pressure, despite the torso's power.
Masters over themselves, they can say: We've come far enough
to know that touching like this is *human*. The gods
exert a stronger pressure on us. But that is *their* way.

If only we too could discover a narrow, purely
human containment, a ribbon of fruitland all to ourselves,
between river and rockface. For our heart still transcends us,
as theirs did. But we can no longer see it embodied
in forms that appease it, or godlike bodies
which manifest it with greater control.

The Third Elegy

It's one thing to celebrate the beloved, but quite another,
the hidden, shameful river-god in the bloodstream.
The beloved only knows the youth from a distance,
and often, before she can soothe him, or as if she didn't exist,
Desire the Master, of whom he knows nothing,
emerges from isolation, to lift up his godhead,
streaming from unknown depths,
arousing the night into endless uproar:
the bloodstream's Neptune, with his terrible trident,
the dark wind of his lungs blown through the spiralled shell.
Listen: the night is moulding and hollowing itself.
But the lover's desire for his beloved's face,
and his inmost insight into its innocence —
don't both come from the innocent stars?

It wasn't your doing, or his mother's either,
that his eyebrows arched with expectation.
And it wasn't for you, the girl who felt their imprint,
that his lips acquired such a sensual curve — not for you.
Do you really believe your soft-footed entry
shocked him so much — when you move like a breeze?
Yes, you jolted his heart; but older terrors
rushed up in him at the shock of that contact.
You call him, but can't quite free him from that dark company.
True, he *wants* to, and does escape; relieved,
he makes himself at home in your heart, and begins himself.
But how could he start from himself?
Mother: *you* made him small; it was you who began him.
For you, he was new, and you curved a friendly world
around his new eyes, and shut out the strangeness.
But now they are gone, the years when your slender figure
would shelter him from the upsurge of chaos.

In this way you hid many things from him; every night
he suspected the bedroom, but you made it harmless,
and out of your heart full of refuge you mixed
a humanized space with his night-space.
Not in the darkness, but in your nearer existence,
you set down the night-light that shone with friendship.
Never a creaking floorboard you didn't explain
as if you already knew when it would happen.
He listened and felt reassured; you effected this
by your quiet departure; behind the wardrobe
his Fate retreated, tall in its cloak, and his turbulent future
merged with the folds of the swaying curtains.

And he himself, as he lay light-hearted
behind the drowsy eyelids you gently shaped,
sweetly dissolving into delicious sleep,
he *seemed* well-protected; but *within,* who was watching
to hinder the primitive inner floods?
There *was* no restraint in the sleeper; he slept,
but gave in to his feverish dreaming.
Untried and uncertain, he soon was entangled
in the spreading offshoots of inner process,
already enmeshed in choking undergrowth,
in bloodthirsty shapes. How he gave in to it. Loved it.
Loved his core, his innermost wilderness,
this primal forest inside him, against whose silent collapse
his heart stood out light green. Loved it. Left it,
emerged from his roots in powerful origin
where his little birth was already outlived.
Loving, he went on down to the older bloodstreams,
down to the canyons where horrors were lying,
still wet from the Fathers. And every horror
acknowledged him, winked in complicity.
Yes, monstrosity smiled. Rarely
have you smiled so sweetly, Mother. How could he

not love it: it smiled at him. He loved it
before you, and when you carried him,
it was already dissolved in the water
supporting the growing embryo.

You see, we're not like the flowers, who love
for only a year; an immemorial sap
comes surging up in our arms when we love.
Listen to this, girl: deep within us, we didn't
love a single future lover, but countless swarms;
not an individual child, but the fathers
who rest in our depths like the ruins of mountains,
and the dried-up riverbed of former mothers,
and the whole of this silent landscape under a clear
or overclouded Fate: all this preceded you, girl.

And you yourself unwittingly summoned
primitive ages up in your lover. What feelings
rose up from those vanished beings. What
women hated you there. What shadowy men
did you rouse in the youth's veins? Dead
children tried to approach you. Gently, gently,
let him rely on your day-work of loving, lead him
close to the garden, counterbalance the nights . . .
Hold him back . . .

The Fourth Elegy

Trees of life: when is your winter?
We're never undivided, instinctive,
like birds migrating. Belated, outstripped,
we suddenly force ourselves on the winds
and drop into indifferent pools. We experience
flowering and withering at the same time.
And somewhere lions still prowl, unconscious,
while their glory lasts, of any weakness.

But we, when we want to focus on one thing completely,
feel it must be at another's expense. Hostility
is close to us. Lovers are always finding
boundaries in each other, instead of
the promised expanses for hunting and homeland.
    For us, even a quick sketch must have
a contrasting background, laboriously prepared,
to make it visible — we need things made explicit.
We do not know our feelings' contours,
only what shapes them from outside.
    Who has not sat in suspense before his heart's curtain?
And up it goes. A goodbye scene.
Easily understood. The familiar garden
wavers slightly. Enter the dancer.
But it's not him. Stop! However smooth his act,
his disguise changes — he becomes a commuter,
entering his house through the kitchen.
    I cannot stand these half-filled masks,
I'd rather have puppets. At least they're full. I can
cope with their stuffing, their strings, and their
faces made of appearance. Here. I am ready.
Even when the lights go out, and they tell me
it's over, and the emptiness comes
off the stage like a drift of grey air;

even when none of my silent forefathers
is sitting beside me, and none of the women —
and not even the boy with the squinting brown eye —
I still stay on. There's always watching.

Am I right? Your life had a bitter flavour,
Father, after you sampled mine,
the first cloudy drops of my destiny;
you continued sampling while I grew up,
and, concerned at the aftertaste of my alien future,
you probed my stricken upturned gaze.
After your death, Father, you've felt like fear
deep within me, within my hopes,
and the wealth of equanimity the dead enjoy,
you've given it up because of my puny Fate,
am I right? And all of you others who loved me
— am I right? — in response to my small beginning
of love for you, which always fell short,
because when I loved the space in your faces
it expanded into world-space, in which
you no longer existed. When I feel like
waiting in front of the puppet-stage, or, rather,
staring so hard that some sort of response
has to emerge to balance my looking, an angel
will come to play and snatch up the strings.
Angel and puppet! Finally a show!
Then what we split by our very existence
comes together. Then, from our various seasons,
the whole transformative cycle emerges
for the first time. Then the angel
is playing above our heads. Look: the dying,
don't they suspect how full of pretence
is all we achieve here? Everything fails
to be itself. At times, in childhood,
more than merely the past was lying behind things,
and ahead was something other than future.
We grew freely, sometimes trying

to grow up faster, half out of love for those
who had nothing more than their grown-up status.
And yet, on our own, we were satisfied
with enduring things, and stood there
in the space between world and toy,
at a place which was, from the beginning,
created for this pure process.

Who shows how it really is with children? Who puts them
among the stars with the yardstick of distances
in their hand? Who makes their death
from grey bread going hard, or leaves it
there in the rounded mouth, like the core
of a beautiful apple? . . . Murderers
are easy to understand. But death,
the *whole* of death — to hold it so gently,
without defiance, even *before* life begins —
this is indescribable.

The Fifth Elegy

But who are they, tell me, these vagrants, a little
more transient even than we are, urgently driven
from early on (for the love of *whom?*)
by some insatiable will? But it wrings them,
bends them, slings them and swings them,
tosses them up and catches them; down they come,
as if out of well-oiled, frictionless air,
onto this carpet worn thin and threadbare
by their endless jumping, this carpet
lost in the universe —
stuck like a plaster to where the suburban
sky has grazed the earth.
                    And barely suggested,
yet upright, there, and on show: Duration's
big initial letter . . . The ever-imminent grip
already bends them, even the strongest men,
just as Augustus the Strong, for a joke at dinner,
would bend a tin plate.

Around this centre,
the Rose of Watching flowers
and sheds its petals. This stamen,
covered in the pollen it sheds, this pistil,
produces the pseudo-fruit of the listless feeling
they're never aware of — glittering with the thinnest
surface of lightest pseudo-smiles.

Here they are: the wizened, wrinkled lifter,
an old hand demoted to drumming now,
shrunken inside his voluminous skin, as if it formerly
held *two* men: one already
laid in the churchyard, the other surviving,
deaf and sometimes a little
weird in his widowed skin.

Then the young man, who looks like the son of a neck
and a nun: skin-tight with muscle
and simple-mindedness.
Oh, and you, who once received as a plaything
a grief, still small, on one of its
lengthy convalescences . . .

And you, who hit the ground
with a thump known only to fruit,
a hundred times daily you fall, unripe,
from the tree built up by the common movement
(a tree which lives through Spring and Summer
and Autumn in no time, faster than water) —
you fall and bounce on the grave.
Sometimes, in a half-pause, a loving look
towards your unloving mother steals
across your face, and dissolves through your body,
whose surface quickly dissipates this shy
and barely tried expression. And again
the man claps his hands for the jump, and before
your grief can mature in your constantly pounding heart,
the soles of your feet are smarting. A few
quick tears are driven into your eyes.
And still, blindly,
you smile . . .

Angel, accept it! Pick this small-flowered healing-herb.
Create a vase to protect it! Put it among the joys
that are *still* not open to us; on a beautiful urn
celebrate it with a flowing floral inscription:
"The Acrobat's Smile."

Then you, my darling,
passed over in silence by the most
desirable joys. Perhaps
your fringes are happy *for* you,
or above your firm young breasts
the green metallic silk feels flattered
and fulfilled. You, the market-fruit
of equanimity, always differently laid
on the balance's swaying scales,
put on display among the shoulders.
Where is the place, somewhere in my heart,
where they could not perform any longer,
and fell apart from each other like mismatched
mating animals;
where weights are too heavy,
and hoops go spinning away
from pointlessly turning sticks . . .

And suddenly this worn-out nowhere becomes
the unbelievable place where sheer insufficiency
turns around to transform itself
into utter superabundance.
Where the sum of many numbers
comes to nothing.

Parisian squares, the infinite showplace
where Madame Lamort, the milliner,
winds and entwines the restless roads of the earth
like endless ribbons, making them into
fresh bows and frills, flowers and cockades,
and artificial fruits, all falsely coloured, for Fate's
cheap winter hats.

Angel: suppose there's a place we don't know, and there,
on an indescribable carpet, lovers can do whatever
they couldn't accomplish here: their eager,
lofty structures of feeling,
their towers of pleasure, their
trembling ladders supporting each other
without any ground; if they were able to do all this
with the countless silent dead as spectators:

    Wouldn't the crowd throw their last, still hoarded,
still hidden, unknown to us, eternally
valid coins of joy, down to the finally
truly smiling couple there on the quieted
carpet?

The Sixth Elegy

Fig-tree: I've always seen a special meaning
in the way you hardly bother to blossom,
but quietly thrust your secret directly
into the timely closure of the fruit.
Like fountain pipes, your supple branches
drive the sap up and down; barely waking, it leaps
straight from sleep to the joy of sweetest achievement.
Look: like Zeus when he entered the swan.
                        . . . But we are slower;
we love to blossom, only belatedly
reaching our final fruition, already betrayed.
Only a few of us feel the urge to action arise so strongly
that they stand at the ready, their hearts full of passion,
when temptation to blossom, like a soft night-breeze,
brushes their youthful lips and eyelids:
heroes, perhaps, and those predestined for early departure,
whose veins are entwined in a special way by Death the Gardener.
They rush ahead, in advance of their smiles,
like the team of horses shown in relief
in the gentle pictures of Karnak the conquering king.

The hero strangely resembles the youthfully dead. Lasting
leaves him indifferent. His upsurge is Being;
he's always venturing into the changed constellation
of his constant danger. Few will discover him there.
But Fate, which darkly silences us, is abruptly inspired
to sing him into the storm of its turbulent world.
Yet I can hear no one as clearly as *him*. His darkened voice
suddenly pierces me, borne on the airstream.
    How much I would like to escape from this longing:
to be a boy who could still be a hero, sitting
secure in the arms of the future, and reading of Samson,
whose mother gave birth to nothing, and finally — All.

Wasn't he a hero inside you already, mother;
didn't his masterful choosing begin there?
Thousands swarmed in your womb, competing to be him,
but watch him: grasping and letting go, choosing and knowing.
And his pulling down pillars happened when he broke
out of the world of your body into the narrower world
where he went on choosing and knowing. Mothers of heroes,
you springs of great rivers, canyons where maidens,
have plunged from the highest heart-brink,
weeping, sacrificed for the future son.

When the hero stormed the emplacements of love,
every heartbeat was meant for him and urged him on,
until he turned to stand beyond the smiles, transformed.

The Seventh Elegy

Enough about love — voice, you've outgrown it;
wooing should not be the nature of your cry, although
it was pure as a bird's when the rising season uplifts it,
almost forgetting its animal worries, a single heart
projected into the brightness of inner heaven.
Even then you were still wooing — hoping you might be
silently sensed by a still invisible lover, whose response
would slowly awaken and warm to your listening,
until she too could feel with your heightened feeling.

And the Spring would understand, and nowhere
would fail to re-echo the note of annunciation. First that little
questioning note, and then, with silence intensified
all around, a purely affirmative day.
Then up the beckoning steps to the dreamed-of
Temple of the Future; and then, like fountain-jets,
music rising and suddenly falling, surprised in the play
of anticipations. And the prospect of Summer.

Not only all of the Summer mornings, the way
they turn into day, radiant even before they begin.
Not only the days, gentle around the flowers,
yet strong and powerful around the shapes of trees.
Not only the prayers of unfolded forces,
not only the paths, the meadows at evening,
the breathing clarity after a recent thunderstorm,
not only the approach of sleep, with a late intuition . . .
but also the nights, the nights of high summer,
and the stars, the stars of the earth.
To die and to know all the stars for ever!
For how, how, how can we ever forget them?

You see how I called up the lover. But *she* might not
come alone . . . Out of their loosening graves, other women
might come and stand . . . For how could I limit
the call once called? The buried always try
to come back to earth. Children: each thing
here on earth is worth understanding.
Believe me, Fate is no more than your childhood intensity.
How often you overtook your sweetheart, out of breath
from happily chasing nothing, into the open air.

Earthly existence is glorious. Even *you* knew this,
women who seem to have missed it, sinking into the worst
alleyways of the city, festering, with open sewers.
For each of you had an hour, perhaps not quite
a whole hour, a gap that can hardly be measured
by our usual measure of time, when you *existed*.
Completely. Existence filled your veins.
But it's easy to forget whatever our smiling neighbour
doesn't acknowledge or envy. *Visible* joy
is what we esteem, although we're only given to know
the *most* visible once we've transformed it within.

Nothing, my love, becomes world except within us.
Our lives are spent on transformation. The outer world
is dwindling all the time. In place of a lasting house,
an abstract, angular structure obtrudes, belonging
completely to theory, as if it still stood in the brain.
The spirit of the age is creating massive reserves of strength,
but formless, like the all-encompassing tension it brings.
Temples are not envisaged. The heart's extravagances
are sparing and secret now. Yet where *one thing* survives,
an object of prayer or worship or service,
it endures, just as it is, in the realm of the invisible.
Many fail to notice, and miss the chance to remake it
within, with pillars and statues, greater!

Every dull turn of the world has its disinherited objects,
no longer part of the past, and not yet part of the future.
For humans, even what's nearest is distant. But we
shouldn't let this disturb us; instead, it should strengthen
awareness of forms we can still acknowledge. This once *stood*
among humans, stood in the midst of destructive Fate,
stood as if it existed, despite our disorientation, and drew
the stars towards it out of the safety of heaven.
Angel, let me show you — it's *there!* Let it stand
in your sight, finally saved and upright for ever.
Pillars, pylons, the Sphinx, and, striving upwards,
grey above a decaying or alien city, the cathedral spire.

Weren't these miracles? Angel, greater than we are,
tell us what we've achieved here — my breath
can hardly sustain this praise. So we haven't yet
completely consumed the endowment of space
we once made our own. (It must have been enormous,
not to have overflowed with the aeons of human feeling.)
But one of our towers was great, wasn't it? Angel, it *was* great,
wasn't it, even next to you? Chartres was great,
and music reached still further beyond us. But even
a woman in love, alone at the window at night,
would reach at least to your knee.
                    Angel, I haven't returned
to wooing. Even if I courted you, you wouldn't come.
For my invocation is full of distance. You couldn't
make headway against so strong a current. My call
is an outstretched arm: the hand is raised and open
for you (beyond our ken) to grasp,
but also a shield and a warning, held high.

The Eighth Elegy

With all their eyes the animals look out
into the Open. Our eyes alone
seem to be turned the other way, like traps
around their outgoing freedom.
Only their faces tell us what *exists*
out there; even young children
we turn around and make them see creation
backwards, and not the Open, lying deep
within the animals' faces. Free of death.
Only *we* see it; the animals are free,
and always keep their deaths behind them,
God in front; and when they run, they run
into eternity, as fountains run.
  Never, even for a single day, do *we*
have pure space before us, where the flowers
open endlessly. It's always world
and never nowhere without nothingness,
pure, unsupervised, which you can breathe
and *know* without desiring it. A child
is sometimes lost in stillness there, but soon
is jolted back. Or someone dies and *is* it.
For, close to death, we no longer *see* death,
because we finally look *outwards* then,
perhaps with the animals' wide open gaze.
Lovers might approach it, full of wonder,
if their partners didn't hide the view.
Each has a glimpse behind the other's back
as if by mistake. But no one can escape
their other, so the world re-forms itself.
Always facing Creation, we can see
only its reflection of the Open,
overshadowed by us. Or when an animal
dumbly looks up, and looks us through and through.

This is our Fate: to be opposite,
and nothing else but always opposite.

If he had consciousness like ours,
the confident animal who meets us
going the other way, would turn us around.
But his Being is unlimited for him,
unformulated, and without regard
for who he is, pure as his outward gaze.
And where we see the future, he sees All,
himself in All, made whole for ever.

And yet the warm and wakeful animal
bears a great weight of melancholy in him.
What often overpowers us can cling
to him as well — a memory that the longed-for state
was nearer once, and truer, infinitely gentle
in its approach. Here, everything stands back.
There we breathed it. After that first home,
the second's windy and precarious.
    How happy are the little animals
who stay within the womb that bore them!
Even on its wedding day, the lucky gnat
still hops *inside* the universal womb.
And look at the half-assurance of the bird,
born with a knowledge of both worlds,
like one of those Etruscan souls
whose dead body lies in a burial chamber,
but whose effigy is resting on the lid.
And for any creature from a womb,
what a shock it is to have to fly. As if
afraid of itself, it penetrates the air
like a crack through a cup. Or a bat's track
fracturing the porcelain of evening.
    And we are always, everywhere, spectators,
focussed *in* on everything, not out.
It overwhelms us. We reconstruct it.

It disintegrates. We reconstruct again.
And then disintegrate ourselves.

Who has turned us around like this,
so that, no matter what we do,
we act like someone just about to leave?
He turns and stops and waits as the last hill
shows him all his valley for the last time —
we live like this, always saying goodbye.

The Ninth Elegy

Why, when our lifespan might be spent
as a laurel, a somewhat darker shade
than all the other green, with little waves
on every leaf-edge, like a breeze's smile —
why do we have to be human, trying
to escape our Fate, but desiring it too?

No, not for the sake of happiness,
this premature profit before a loss,
or curiosity, or to train the heart —
these would exist in the laurel too.

But because being here means so much, and because
all of the transient things that are here
seem to need us — this strangely concerns us.
They need us — *us,* the most transient. *Once*
for each thing, just once. Once and no more.
Just once for us too. Never again. But having been
earthly just this once, even though
it was only once, seems irrevocable.

And so we force ourselves and want to achieve it,
want to contain it within our simple hands,
our overflowing gaze and our speechless heart.
Want to become it. To give it to whom? We'd like to
keep it all for ever — but what can we take across
to the other dimension? Not seeing, the art we've slowly
acquired here, nothing that's happened here. Nothing.
Even the suffering. Even the sadness.
Even the long experience of loving.
They're unsayable. Later, under the stars,
what then? They're *better* unsayable.
What does the wanderer bring from the mountain-slopes

back to the valley? Not a handful of inarticulate earth,
but a word he's discovered, the yellow and blue
gentian. Perhaps we are here just to say: House,
Bridge, Fountain, Gate, Jug, Fruit-tree, Window —
and most of all: Pillar, Tower. But to *say* them, you see,
in a way that the things themselves had never
inwardly meant to be. Is this the hidden design
of the cunning earth in encouraging lovers:
to thrill each part of itself through their feelings?
Threshold: what does it matter if two
lovers wear away the doorstep a little
behind the many who went ahead
and those who are still to come . . . quietly.

Here is the time of the sayable, here is its homeland.
Speak and acknowledge it. More than ever,
the things we experience are falling away,
forcibly ousted by acts without imagination.
Acts under crusts that easily crumble, as soon as
the inner motive weakens and finds other forms.
Between the hammers, the heart
survives, like the tongue
between the teeth, still
persisting with praise.

Praise *this world* to the angel, not the unsayable.
Your rapturous feelings cannot impress him; in the cosmos,
where his feelings are felt more intensely, you're merely a novice.
So show him a simple thing, formed over generations,
which lives in our hands and our eyes like one of us.
Say *things* to him. He'll stand there astonished, as you did
by the ropemaker in Rome or the potter beside the Nile.
Show him how happy a thing can be, how guiltless and ours.
How even the pain of grief can be purified into form,
serve as a thing, die *into* a thing — transcending
the violin. And these things, which live on passing away,
are aware of your praising them; transient,

they trust to us for their rescue, *us,* the most transient.
Want to be fully transformed into *us,* forever,
inside our invisible hearts. Whoever we finally are.

Earth, is this what you want: *invisible*
resurrection within us? Is this your dream,
to be invisible? Earth! Invisible!
What is your urgent demand, if not transformation?
Earth, I love you, I will. Believe me, I need
no more of your Springs to convince me. *One,*
a single one, is already too much for my blood.
You've always had my utter devotion.
You've always been right, and your sacred intuition
is intimate Death.

Look, I'm alive. On what? Neither childhood nor future
diminish . . . Superabundant being
springs up in my heart.

The Tenth Elegy

At the outcome of all these harrowing insights,
let my jubilant praise be in tune with the angels.
Let none of the clear-struck keys of my heart
fail on a wavering, slack or snapping string.
Let the tears streaming down my face
make me more radiant; let the invisible tears
blossom. How precious you'll be to me, Nights,
in my grief. Why didn't I greet you by kneeling lower,
disconsolate sisters, lose myself more
in your loosened hair? We waste our sorrows.
We look beyond them into the sadness of time
to see if they end. But they are really
our winter foliage, our dark evergreen,
one of our secret seasons — no, more than that —
they are place, plot, hearth, earth, home.

But how strange they are, the streets of the City of Pain,
where, in the false silence created by sounds
drowning each other out, the banal and pompous memorial,
poured from the mould of vacuity, makes its gilded din.
An angel would trample to pieces their market of comforts
next to the church they bought ready-made, now clean
and disappointingly closed as the Post Office on Sunday.
But right outside is the rippling fringe of the fairground.
Swings of freedom! Eager jugglers and divers!
And dolled-up Luck's life-like shooting-gallery,
with flapping targets, and rattling tin
when a marksman scores. From handclaps to mishaps
he staggers on, for booths to suit every fancy
entice and wheedle and clamour. "For adults only,
a special attraction: seeing how money reproduces,
anatomically shown, not just entertainment:
the sexual organ of money, the whole process,

uncensored, educational, enhances
fertility . . ."
        But just beyond, behind the last hoarding
plastered with posters for EVERLIFE,
the bitter beer that tastes great to drinkers
as long as they're munching on fresh distractions —
right behind the hoarding, right behind, begins the Real.
Children are playing, and lovers holding each other, private,
earnest, on the thin grass, while dogs act out their nature.
The young man is drawn further on: perhaps he's in love
with a Sorrow . . . He walks behind her into the meadows.
"It's a long way," she tells him. "We live over there." Where?
The young man follows, touched by her manner.
Her shoulders and neck . . . perhaps she's of noble family.
And yet he leaves her, turns around, heads back,
waves goodbye . . . What does it matter? She's only a Sorrow.

Only those who die young, who are still
in the first timeless calm after weaning,
follow her lovingly. Young women
she waits for, befriends them.
Shows them quietly what she is wearing.
Pearls of grief and delicate
veils of patience. With young men
she walks in silence.

But there, where they live, in the valley, an older Sorrow
takes the young man on and answers his questions. She says:
"We were a noble family once, we Sorrows. The Fathers
carried out mining up on the mountain: sometimes
you find a nugget of carved-out pain among humans,
or, from an ancient volcano, the slag of petrified anger.
That's where it came from. Once we were rich . . ."

And gently she leads him over the landscape of Sorrow,
shows him the pillars of temples, or the ruins
of cities where Princes of Sorrow once
wisely ruled the land. Shows him the high
trees of weeping, the fields of blossoming grief
(seen by the living only as pleasant foliage);
shows him the beasts of mourning grazing — and sometimes
a startled bird takes flight across their view,
trailing the long inscription of its lonely cry.
In the evening she brings him up to the graves
of the tribal ancestors, sybils and augurers.
But night is nearing, so they walk more softly,
and soon it towers up, the Tombstone
that watches over the world. Twin of the Nile's
noble Sphinx — the silent inner chamber's face.
In amazement they look at the royal head,
which silently sets the human face
on the scale of the stars for ever.

His eyes cannot take it in, still dazed
from recent death. But a look from her
rouses an owl from behind the rim of the crown,
where the rounding is ripest, faintly inscribing
onto his hearing, still fresh from death,
like the facing pages of a newly opened book,
the indescribable outline.

And higher still, the stars. New ones.
Stars of the land of pain. Slowly, the Sorrow
names them: "Look: the Rider, the Staff,
and that denser constellation is called
the Garland of Fruit. Further, near to the Pole,
Cradle, Pathway, the Burning Book, Doll, Window.
But there in the southern sky, pure as if held
in the palm of a holy hand, the clearly shining M
that stands for Mothers . . ."

But the dead man has to continue, and the older Sorrow
brings him down to the canyon,
where, shimmering in the moonlight,
is the wellspring of joy. With reverence
she names it, and tells him, "For humans,
this is a nurturing stream."

They stand at the foot of the mountain.
And there she hugs him, weeping.
Alone, he marches into the mountains of primal pain.
And no footstep rings out of his silent Fate.

But if they wanted to give us a likeness,
the numberless dead might point to the catkins
hanging from empty hazel-trees, or the rain
falling on darkened earth in the Spring.

And we, who think of happiness
as *rising*, would feel so moved
we would almost faint
if it started to *fall*.

THE SONNETS TO ORPHEUS

—

Part One

1

A tree rose up. O pure transcendence!
Orpheus is singing! O high tree in the ear!
And all fell silent. Yet even in the silence
new beginnings, changes, signs appeared.

Creatures from stillness crowded from the clear
untangled forest out of lair and nest.
Then it emerged that neither fear
nor cunning kept them all so quiet,

but listening. Bellow, screech, and roar
shrank in their hearts. And where
scarcely a hut received all this before —

merely a tunnel of obscure desire,
with shaking timbers at its door —
you made them temples in their hearing.

2

It was almost a girl, and appeared
out of this unity of song and lyre,
and through her springtime veils shone clear,
and came to rest embedded in my ear.

And slept in me. Her sleep *was* everything:
the trees I always marvelled at, and these
tangible distances, the touch of fields,
and anything I found astonishing.

Singing god, she slept the world.
You made her perfect, so she had no need
to stay awake. She rose and fell asleep.

Where is her death? And can you improvise
her death-theme now, before your singing dies?
Falling away from me . . . Almost a girl . . .

3

A god can. But how can humans follow,
tell me, through the narrow lyre?
Our mind is split. Where heartways cross,
there never stands a temple to Apollo.

You teach that song is not desire
for *having* something in the end:
song is *being*. Easy for a god.
But when do *we* exist? And when

does he centre earth and stars on *our* being?
No, it's *not* when you're in love, young lover,
although your voice burst from your mouth —

learn to forget that outcry. It expires. To sing
in truth is quite a different breath.
For nothing. A breath of god. A wind.

4

Loved ones: enter now and then
this breath, not really meant for you;
let your cheeks divide it into two,
and it trembles behind you, united again.

You who are blessed, you who are whole,
who seem to be the beginning of hearts.
Bows for the arrows and also the targets,
your tearful smiles shine more eternal.

Don't be afraid to suffer: the burden,
give it back to the weight of the earth;
heavy the mountains, heavy the seas.

Even the trees you planted as children
finally grew too heavy; you couldn't bear them.
But the open spaces . . . but the breeze . . .

5

Don't raise a monument. Just let the roses
bloom year after year in his honour.
For it is Orpheus. His metamorphosis
in this one and in this. No need to bother

with other names. It's *Orpheus,* always,
whenever there's singing. He comes and goes.
Isn't it enough if he outstays the rose
in the rosebowl, at times, by a few days?

How he must vanish so you understand!
Fearful though he is to disappear.
Just as his words surpass existence here,

he's gone beyond your reach already.
The lyre's trellis doesn't tie his hand.
And he obeys by overstepping.

6

Is he from *this* world? No,
his broader nature grew from *both.*
One who has known the roots below
will better bend the willow boughs.

When you go to bed, don't leave the bread
or milk on the table: they attract the dead.
Rather, let *him,* the conjuror, instead
under the mildness of your eyelids blend

their apparition into everything you see;
and let the spell of earthsmoke and rue
be as true for him as the clearest relation.

Nothing spoils the valid symbol for him:
whether found in graves or in rooms,
let him praise jug and clasp and ring.

7

Praise is the task! Summoned to praise,
he ran like ore from out of the stone's
silence. His heart, the transient press
of unending wine for man.

The dust never makes his voice give out
when the god's example grips.
All becomes vineyard and grapes,
ripened in his passionate south.

Decay in royal crypts does not
refute his praising, nor
that a shadow falls from the gods.

He is a messenger who stays
far behind death's door
holding bowls of fruit worth praise.

8

Only in Praise's precincts can she walk,
Grief, the nymph of the weeping well;
she watches over our stream of tears,
to keep it clear to the very rock

that bears the gateways and the altars.
Look: the feeling she's the youngest-born
among the spirit's sisterhood of moods
dawns around her quiet shoulders.

Joy *knows,* and Longing is stilled —
only Grief continues learning: night by night
her girlish hands count up old ills.

But suddenly, awkward and unskilled
she holds our voice's constellation high
into the sky unclouded by her breath.

9

Only one who raised his lyre
among the shades,
may perform, inspired,
the endless praise.

Only one who ate
their poppy with the dead,
will find his faintest note
can never fade.

Although the reflection often
dissolves in the water:
know the image.

Only in the double kingdom
do voices soften
and last for ever.

10

You, who never leave my feelings,
welcome, ancient sarcophagi,
where Roman days flow happily,
like a wandering song.

Or those that are as open-eyed,
as a happy shepherd waking up —
full of stillness and nettles inside,
and butterflies fluttering above.

All who are snatched from doubt,
I welcome, re-opened mouths,
who know what silence is about.

Friends, can *we* understand,
or not? Slow Time marks both
on the face of man.

11

Look at the sky. Isn't a constellation there
called "Rider"? (It's strangely impressed on us,
this pride of earth.) And a second one, thus:
driving and holding him, and whom he bears.

Spurred on and then reined in — isn't it thus,
the resilient nature of our being?
Straight on, then turning. Attuned by a touch.
New distances. And the two are one.

But *are* they? Or is the meaning of both
only the way which they travel together?
Table and pasture divide them completely.

Even their union in the stars is deceiving.
But let us be glad for a while believing
in the figure. That is enough.

12

Welcome, spirit that can unite us;
for living through symbols is our truest way.
And clocks take little steps beside us,
missing our authentic day.

We do not know our real place,
yet act from true affinity.
Antennae answering antennae,
and out of empty space . . .

Pure tension! Music of the powers!
And yet we hide from every tremor
with all these petty tasks of ours.

Even for the farmer scraping to live,
the place where seed becomes summer
is out of reach. The earth *gives*.

13

Ripe apple, raspberry, and pear,
banana . . . All of them pronounce
life and death inside the mouth.
A child's face: you can read it there,

the taste. This comes from far away.
Isn't your mouth dumbfounded slowly?
In place of words, discoveries flow
out of the fruit-flesh by surprise.

Dare to say what you call "an apple."
The sweetness, first of all condensed,
then, in the tasting, more intense,

emerges clear, transparent, wakeful,
ambiguous, sunny, earthy, local . . .
Oh life, experience, joy — immense!

14

We are in touch with flowers, vine leaves, fruit.
Their speech exceeds the language of the year.
Out of the dark, a bright display appears,
which has perhaps an envious glint

from those who fortify the earth: the dead.
What do we know about the role they play?
For ages their way has been to spread
their liberated marrow through the clay.

The question is: do they *want* to? Are these fruits
the work of sullen slaves, pushed up at us,
the masters, like fists in our faces?

Are *they* the masters, who sleep among the roots,
and grant us from their surpluses
this mixture of their silent strength and kisses?

15

Wait . . . that wonderful taste . . . already faint.
Let's have some music — let's stamp and hum!
Girls, you eager ones, girls, you shy ones: come
and dance the taste you knew in the fruit!

Dance the orange. Who could forget it,
how, drowning in itself, it is shy
of its own sweetness. But you possessed it.
It has turned into you, deliciously.

Dance the orange. That warmer scene,
project it from you, so ripeness may shine
in its homeland breezes! Glowing, let loose

waves of your fragrance. Identify
with the pure, reluctant-clinging rind,
and the luscious fruit's abundant juice!

16

You, my friend, are lonely because . . .
We, with our finger-pointing and words,
gradually appropriate the world —
perhaps the weakest part, the most dangerous.

No one points a finger at a smell.
But you sense many of the threats
around us . . . You recognize the dead
and cower at their magic spell.

Look: together now we have to understand
the bits and pieces as the whole.
It will be hard to help you. Most of all,

don't plant me in your heart. I'd grow too well.
But I will guide *my* master's hand,
and say: Here. This is Esau in his pelt.

17

Deepest of all: the ancient, tangled
root of all that's grown,
hidden spring
they'd never known.

Helmet and hunting-horn,
greybeard wisdom,
rage between brothers-born,
lute-like women.

Branches fight in the tree,
without one getting free . . .
But *one* is climbing, higher!

Still they go on breaking.
But the top one is bending
into a lyre.

18

Master: can you hear the New
droning and drumming?
Prophets are coming
to herald it, too.

No one can truly hear
in the deafening noise,
and yet the machines appear
to demand our praise.

The Machine: observe
its vengeful churning action
distort and weaken our lives.

Though its energy derives
from us, let it work and serve
without our passion.

19

The world may change as fast
as the shape of clouds,
but everything perfect at last
falls home to the age-old.

Above all passing and change,
freer and wider,
your prelude-song remains,
god with the lyre.

We don't know how to grieve,
and haven't learned to love;
what carries us far off

in death is not revealed.
Only the song above
the land can bless and heal.

20

But what shall I offer you, Master, say —
who taught all creatures to hear?
My memory of a springtime day,
at evening, in Russia, a horse . . .

Across from the village the horse came alone,
with one of his legs in a fetter,
to spend the night in the fields on his own;
how the locks of his mane all together

beat on his neck in the passionate rhythm
of that crudely constricted gallop!
How his horse's blood rose up!

He sensed the distances, sang and listened!
Your mythic cycle was closed *within* him.
I offer you this: his image.

21

Spring has come back again. The earth
is a child who knows many poems by heart . . .
For the long, hard work of learning
she now receives the prize.

Her teacher was strict. But we loved the white
in the old man's beard. Now if we ask her
what the green and the blue are called,
she always gets the answer right.

The earth is joyful, on holiday, having fun
with the children. You'll be caught,
happy earth, by the happiest one.

Everything that her teacher taught,
everything printed in roots and long
and difficult stems, she recites in a song!

22

We are the driving force.
But Time's passing
has little importance
in the everlasting.

All that urgency
will soon be past;
for permanency
baptized us first.

Boys, don't put your best
into trial flight
or speed. Look:

all is at rest.
Darkness and light.
Flower and book.

23

Only *then:* when flight
climbs up the silent sky
for *more* than sheer delight
in being able to fly,

letting its bright profiles play,
the darling of the winds,
a triumphant toy,
supple, secure, and slim —

only when a purer quest
outweighs this boyish pride
in feats of technology,

will the pilot, wild with success,
and near the horizon, *be*
the goal of his solo flight.

24

Should we reject our age-old friends, the great
and never-importunate gods, because they're ignored
by the hard steel we so strictly brought up —
or suddenly search for them on a map?

These powerful friends, who receive our dead,
never touch our wheels. Our baths, our festivals
are far removed from them now. Instead,
we're always overtaking their messengers,

long since too slow for us. Lonelier, turning
only towards each other, though still unknown
to each other, we build straight roads

without lovely curves. The former fires are burning
only in boilers, lifting bigger and bigger hammers.
But we are losing strength, like swimmers.

25

But now it is *you*, whom I knew as a nameless flower,
it is *you* I'll recall and show them just *one* more time,
you who departed early, beautiful,
at play with the irrepressible cry.

First as a dancer, suddenly standing apart,
like a bronze cast of her own youth, grieving
and listening. From the dancers' achieving,
music fell into her altered heart.

Illness was near. The shadows had overpowered
her bloodstream, but, as if only briefly in doubt,
it surged back into its natural springtime state.

Again and again, interrupted by darkness and downfall,
it shone with life. Until after terrible pounding
it entered the desolate open gate.

26

But you, divine one, sang to the end, when the horde
of rejected Maenads attacked you. Beautiful,
you sounded above their clamour with order;
from among the destroyers arose your uplifting music.

None of them there could crush your head or your lyre,
however they wrestled and raged, and all of the sharp
stones they hurled at your heart
went soft as they reached you, and could hear.

At last they dismembered you, hot for revenge,
while your sounds lingered on in lions and cliffs,
and in birds and trees. You are singing there still.

You lost god! You infinite trace!
Only since enmity tore you apart are we now
your hearers, and one of Nature's mouths.

Part Two

1

Breathing, you invisible poem!
World-space in constant interchange
with itself. Counterweight
in which I rhythmically become.

Single wave,
I am your gradual
sea, the thriftiest possible:
saving of space.

How many places in space were once
inside me. Many a wind
is like a son.

Do you know me, air, full of places that were
once mine? You once smooth rind,
rounding and leaf of my words.

2

Just as the nearest piece of paper
sometimes receives the artist's *real*
master-stroke, so mirrors often capture
the sacred, solitary smile

of girls trying out the morning alone,
or the flattering candlelight. And later,
in the breathing of their own faces,
only a reflection's shown.

How we've stared into the sooty hearth,
and its slowly dying glow:
glimpses of life, lost beyond recall.

Who can know the losses of the earth?
Only the singer, who, even so,
praises the heart, reborn into the All.

3

Mirrors: no one yet has managed to give
a true account of what your essence is.
You, time's interstices,
as full of holes as a sieve.

You, still emptying the empty hall
when, wide as forests, dusk is near . . .
And the antlers of the chandelier
leap through your impenetrable wall.

At times you're full of painting. A few
figures seem to have entered you,
while others you gently set aside.

But the greatest beauty stays and waits,
until released Narcissus penetrates
to her cheeks, which you retain inside.

4

This is the animal that doesn't exist.
Unaware of this, they loved him anyway:
his neck, his movements' grace,
and the light in his peaceful gaze.

In fact, he *was* not. Yet, because
they loved him, a pure creature came to be.
They always left him room. And in the space
they cleared, he raised his head so easily

he hardly needed to exist. No grain
was fed him, just the chance to be.
This made him strong enough to grow a horn

out of his forehead. Only one.
Appearing to a virgin, white, he *was*
in the silver-mirror and in her.

5

Flower-muscle, making the anemone
slowly open to the morning meadowland,
until the sky's polyphony
of light pours down into your lap;

muscle of infinite receptiveness,
tense within the quiet blossom-star,
sometimes overwhelmed so far
with fullness that sunset's call to rest

can hardly give the wide-uncurled
petal-edges back to you:
you, the will and strength of many worlds.

We, the powerful, are longer-living.
But *when*, in all that life, are we
as open and receiving?

6

Royal rose: in ancient times you were
a chalice with a single rim.
Today you are a many-petalled flower,
an infinitely complex thing.

In your richness you shine like layers
of clothing around a body of light;
yet all clothing is banished and denied
by a single petal of yours.

For centuries your scent has called
its sweetest names across to us;
suddenly it's in the air, like fame.

But we can only guess its name . . .
And memory is drawn to it
from moments still in our recall.

7

Flowers, relatives of the hands that arrange you
(hands of girls of long ago and now),
often you cover the garden table
drooping, lightly wounded, waiting

for water to bring you back from a death
already begun, and now returning to life
between the streaming poles of feeling fingers
which are able to do you more good than you thought,

you light ones, when you came round in the jug,
shedding the warmth of the girls
like confessions, like burdensome sins

committed by your being plucked,
and reconnecting you to those
who unite with you in blossoming.

8

You children — only a few — who played with me
in the scattered city parks of long ago,
how we'd find and befriend each other shyly,
and, like the lamb with the speaking scroll,

talk silently. If we were happy,
it belonged to no one. Whose could it be?
But it melted among the passers-by
and the long year's anxiety.

Carriages rolled around us, alien. Stark,
but unreal, the houses ringed us. And none
ever knew us. What *was* real in it all?

Nothing. Only the balls. Their wonderful arcs.
Not even the children. But sometimes one
stepped briefly under the falling ball.

In memoriam Egon von Rilke

9

Judges, don't pride yourselves, please,
on getting rid of the neck-iron and rack.
No heart is moved because a self-induced attack
of mercy gave you a gentle squeeze.

The scaffold surrenders all that it gained
over the ages, like children giving back
their last year's birthday toys. He'd enter the gate
of the open heart in a different way,

the god of true mercy. He'd come more strongly to grips,
reach more radiantly round him, more godlike.
More than a wind for the great protected ships.

A gentle, secret, inner awareness,
silently winning us, like a quietly playing child,
born of immortal parents.

10

The machine is a threat to all we have won,
if it invades the spirit and fails to obey.
It's ousted handicraft's slower, lovelier way
with starker buildings, and harsher cutting of stone.

We *never* escape it — it never stays
in the factory, oily and self-possessed.
It's life itself, and thinks it knows best
because it impartially orders, creates and destroys.

.

But life is still magic for us; at hundreds
of places it is still origin. No one can know
this field of power and fail to kneel in wonder.

Before the unsayable, language still fades out . . .
And Music, choosing the most vibrating stones,
builds in unusable space her deified house.

11

Many calmly administered systems of death
have existed in human progress since hunting started.
But better known to me than trap or net
is the canvas strip they dangled into the caves of the Karst.

They lowered it gently, like a peace-sign.
But then the boy twitched the end, and the night
threw a handful of pale and tumbling pigeons
out of the caves into daylight . . . But even *this* is right.

Onlookers need not sigh with pity,
any more than the hunter, whose watchful skill
performs what is timely. *To kill*

is a form of our wandering sorrow . . .
Whatever we undergo
is pure to the serene spirit.

12

Will transformation. Be inspired by the flame
where something elusively flaunts its changing.
The shaping spirit which governs the earthly
prefers the turning-point most in the flux of form.

What is confined to surviving already *is* rigid;
does it think itself safe under cover of neutral grey?
Wait: the hardened are warned from far away
by the hardest: an absent hammer is lifted!

Awareness acknowledges those who flow like springs,
and leads them entranced through the bright creation,
where beginnings often end, and endings begin.

Every beautiful space they cross, amazed, is an offspring,
child or grandchild, of Separation.
And Daphne, now laurel, wants *you* to turn into wind.

13

Anticipate every parting; put it behind you,
like the Winter now leaving. For there will arrive
an infinite Winter, and if you come through,
your heart will always survive.

Always be dead in Eurydice — singing
and praising more, rise to that purer state.
Here, in this realm of decay, be a ringing
glass that shattered as it rang.

Be — at the same time know non-existence,
the infinite ground of your inner vibration,
so that you fully perfect it just this once.

To the used as well as the muffled and dumb
stores of full Nature, the endless accumulation,
joyfully add yourself and cancel the sum.

14

Look at the flowers, the earth's faithful:
we lend them Fate from Fate's very edge.
But who knows? If they regret their fading,
it is up to us to *be* their regret.

All has a will to change. But we are heavy,
and lay our selves all around, enjoying our weight.
What exhausting teachers for things we make,
while they are blessed with childhood for ever.

If one could take them into his deepest sleep,
sleep deeply with things, how lightly he'd step,
another into another day, out of the communal deep.

Or perhaps he'd stay, and they'd blossom for him,
praise him, their convert, now like one of them,
all the still children out in the fields and the wind.

15

Fountain-mouth, you giver, source
of one unbroken flow of speech —
covering the water's liquid face,
a marble mask. Behind you reach

the aqueducts. They bring you all you say:
from the slope of the Appenines,
passing by graveyards on its way
and falling over your blackened chin

into the basin set below you here.
This is the sleeping, outspread ear,
the marble ear you always speak into.

An ear of earth's. And so she's just
talking to herself. If you
pushed in a jug, you'd interrupt.

16

Again and again, we tear it up,
but the god is the healing place.
Our will to knowledge sharpens us,
but he is diffused and at peace.

Even the offering of pure devotion
he only receives into his world
by placing himself, without emotion,
opposite the open end.

We only *hear* the spring,
but they can drink as well,
at the god's silent bidding: the dead.

We are offered the sound instead.
And the lamb begs for his bell
from a quieter instinct.

17

Where, in what happily watered gardens, on what trees,
among what gently falling blossom-chalices,
ripen the exotic fruits of consolation? These delicacies —
perhaps you'll find one in the trampled field

of your destitution. Time after time,
you're struck by the size of the fruit,
its soundness, the smoothness of the rind,
and that a bird's whim or a worm's spite

didn't spoil it first. Are there trees so full of angels,
tended by slow and secret gardeners so strangely,
that they bear us fruit without being ours?

The way we ripen too soon and decay,
we shadows and shades, cannot take away
the equanimity of those calm summers.

18

Dancer, you transposition
of transience into movement: you achieved it here.
And the final spin, that tree out of motion,
didn't it fully possess the turning year?

Didn't the tree-top, to centre your spinning,
suddenly blossom from stillness? And over it, too,
wasn't the sun, the summer, the infinite
warmth, created by you?

But it also bore, your tree of ecstasy.
Aren't these its peaceful fruits: the jug, striped
as it ripened, and the riper vase?

And in the pictures: isn't there still the trace,
the dark stroke your eyebrows quickly inscribed
on the wall of their own turning?

19

Somewhere inside the obsequious bank
lives Gold, on familiar terms with many.
But with that blind beggar, even a copper penny
feels lost, like the dusty corner under the wardrobe.

Money's at home in all of the stores,
costumed in silks and furs and carnations.
But the silent beggar stands in the pause
of Money's constant breathing, asleep or waking.

How does it close at night, this ever-open hand?
Tomorrow Fate will fetch it again, and daily
will hold it out: vulnerable, abject, clear.

Will someone with *sight* at last understand,
and praise its endurance? Only a singer can say it.
Only a god can hear.

20

How far between the stars; yet how much further
the distances down here.
Even between one child and another
is inconceivably far.

Perhaps Fate measures us against the span
of Being, and that seems alien.
Think of the spans between woman and man
when she desires and avoids him.

Everything is distant — the circle cannot close.
Look at the dish on the dinner table:
strange, the fish's face.

Fish cannot speak . . . we thought. Who knows?
Somewhere perhaps we may be able
to speak their language *in their place.*

21

Sing, my heart, about gardens you've never known,
bright and remote, like gardens set in glass.
Water and roses of Isfahan and Shiraz,
sing their praises, second to none.

Show, my heart, that you will always be there.
That they have you in mind, their ripening figs.
That you blend among the blossoms and twigs
with the intensified, near-visible air.

Never make the mistake of believing
you have to renounce in order to be!
Silk thread: you too went into the weaving.

Whichever image expresses your mind,
even a scene from a life of misery,
feel the whole carpet's radiant design!

22

In spite of Fate: the glorious overflow
of our existence, foaming up
into parks, or stone figures below
high archways supporting balconies!

Or the bronze bell that lifts its tongue
daily against everyday dullness.
Or there in Karnak, the column, the *one*,
outliving near-eternal temples.

But now the same excesses rush away
as speed, out of the level yellow day
into the dazzled, scattered night.

The frenzy disappears without a trace.
Perhaps they're not in vain, these flights
and their pilots. Yet only as thought.

23

Call me to the one among your hours
that unremittingly resists you — near
and pleading like the face of a dog,
but always seeming to disappear

when you think you've got it finally.
What eludes you — that is most your own.
We're free. But where we thought we'd be
most welcome, we only found rejection.

Anxiously we hanker for a hold,
we, who are often too young for the old,
and too old for what never was.

We only do justice where we praise,
for we are both the branch and the blade
and the sweetness of ripening danger.

24

This urge, always new, out of broken clay!
The first adventurers had few supporters.
Yet cities still arose on beautiful bays,
and pitchers were filled with oil and water.

We eagerly project the gods in thought;
then hostile Fate destroys it all again.
But they are the Immortals. Look: we ought
to hear him out, who'll hear us in the end.

For thousands of years we've been one race,
mothers and fathers full of a future
child who will bury us later and take our place.

How much time we have to be ventured in!
And only silent Death knows who we are,
and knows, investing us, what he'll win.

25

Already, listen, you hear the first plough
at work; human rhythm returns
in the breathless silence of the earth,
tense with early Spring. And now

what's coming seems untasted to you.
It's come so many times before,
yet still seems new. Always hoped for,
you never grasped it. It grasped you.

Even wintered oakleaves shine
at evening with a future brown.
Sometimes breezes exchange a sign.

The bushes are black. Yet heaps of dung
spread a richer black on the ground.
In passing, each hour grows young.

26

How bird-cries strike us . . .
Or any other outcry.
But the children, at play outside —
they already cry past real cries.

Cry Fate. Into the gaps of world-space
(which swallow bird-cries like dreams
engulfing dreamers) they force
their wedges of screams.

Where are we? Freer than ever,
we're like loose kites chasing around
in mid-air, with edges of laughter

frayed by the wind. Order these criers,
singing god, so they rise and resound,
a stream to bear the head and the lyre.

27

Does he really exist, Time the Destroyer?
When will he smash the castle on its peaceful hill?
And this heart, that belongs to the gods for ever,
can the Demiurge overpower it at will?

Are we really so anxiously fragile
as Fate would like us to feel?
Does the deep-rooted promise of childhood
later die unfulfilled?

Ah, transience's ghost,
through the openly receiving,
passes like smoke.

And yet our endless striving
still counts among the surviving
powers the gods invoke.

28

Come and go . . . You, almost a child still,
extend for a moment your dance's pattern
into the pure constellation of one of those
dances in which we fleetingly excel

Nature's dull order. For she roused herself
to full hearing only when Orpheus played.
You were still moved by that event,
slightly offended if a tree delayed

in following you on the way to hear.
You still knew the place where the lyre
rose sounding — the unheard-of centre.

For this you learned your beautiful steps:
to turn your friend to face and walk
towards the sacred celebration.

29

Silent friend of many distances, feel
how space is still increasing through
your breath. Among dark belfries' beams,
let yourself ring out. What's eating you

will grow strong on this food.
Transform yourself, time after time.
What was the worst experience for you?
Was drinking bitter? Be the wine.

Be, in this night's immensity,
magic at the crossroad of your senses — be
their strange encounter's meaning. And,

if the earthly has forgotten you,
say to the still Earth: I flow.
And tell the flowing stream: I am.

SELECTED LAST POEMS

We've listened to fountains so long,
they sound to us almost like time.
But they are rather keeping step
with changing eternity.

Their water is other, yet also yours;
from here, yet also elsewhere;
for a while you are the fountain-basin,
and things are reflected in *you*.

Everything's far away, yet related,
deciphered, yet still unknown,
meaningless, then meaningful again.

So love the things you do not know.
Accepting the gift of your feeling,
they carry it off — who knows where?

That nothing is ever lost to us,
that even those who wish to destroy
out of impatience, are forced to create
again and again out of the whole
fullness. Even those who destroy . . .

Silence. Whoever has been silent
inwardly, touches the roots of speech.
Each developed syllable then
brings him a victory over

what is not silent in silence,
over disdainful evil.
The Word was given to him
to lose it without a trace.

Give your heart a sign
that the winds are changing.
If this is seen by the gods,
hope is unsurpassed.

Rise up and hold still
in the great relatedness;
rigidity gently melts,
mildly the bow disappears.

Cracks appear in the walls
of your long-inhabited Fate,
and a more compassionate moon
shines in the strongest prison.

Even our losses are *ours;* and even forgetting
retains a shape in the permanent realm of transformation.
What we have lost still circulates, and though we are seldom
the circle's centre, that sacred form is still drawn around us.

A blackbird in November sounded
like music glancing in a mirror,
or someone touching his hair
because a lover stroked it once.

But on a February morning
a finch already dares to speak
something *other* than a memory
out into the open year.

Early Spring

Harshness disappeared. Reprieve now lies
on the fields' ploughed-up grey.
Water-trickles change their intonation.
Vague endearments from the skies

drift earthwards. Pathways lead
far inland and point to it.
Unexpectedly, you see its rise
prefigured in the empty tree.

Transience

Quicksand of time. Quiet, persistent crumbling
even of buildings blessed with good luck.
Life breathes on. Disconnected pillars,
supporting nothing, tower upwards.

But why should decay be sadder than
a fountain's return to its shimmering mirror?
Let us persist in the teeth of Change,
until its seeing head has fully grasped us.

Already sap returns to the light
from everything darkly renewed
at the roots, and feeds the pure green
which rinds still shield from the wind.

The inside of Nature revives itself,
secreting a new rejoicing;
the whole year's youth, as yet unnoticed,
rises into the stiffening branches.

The glorious shape of the old nut-tree,
outwardly cool and grey, is full of future;
the youthful thickets shiver with tension
at the premonitions of the little birds.

Walk

My look's already at the sunlit hill
ahead on the road I've just begun.
Thus what we cannot grasp, grasps *us,*
from far away, in full epiphany,

and changes us, without our reaching it,
to what, unknowing, we already are;
our sign is answered by a counter-sign.
But we can only feel the counter-wind.

Streams enrapture the land.
A breathlessly drinking Spring
stumbles blindly into the greenery,
and forces its drunken breath
through the mouths of the blossoms.

The nightingales practise all day
to celebrate their feelings,
and their overwhelming power
over the sober stars.

Joy, restrained for much too long, breaks free
so strongly, it overruns the fields;
and Summer, like a giant stretching, feels
the vigour of its youth in the old nut-tree.

The lightweight blossoms soon drifted away;
more serious green got to work in the trees;
how spaces curved around each of them,
and how much tomorrow lived in each today.

Do you still remember: falling stars
raced across the sky like horses,
clearing the sudden barriers —
why so many? — put up by our desires,
and countless stars sprang out;
almost every glance was wedded
to the quick daring of their play;
the heart felt whole among these shards
of radiance, and was healed
as if it had outlived them.

Just as Nature surrenders beings
to the venture of their blind desire,
without any special protection
in the soil or among the branches:
so we ourselves are no more precious
to our being's Ground: *it ventures us.*
It's just that, more than plants and animals,
we go along with it, this venturing,
and will it, sometimes more adventurous
(and not from egotism) than Life itself,
more daring by a breath . . . And this creates for us
a place of safety, far beyond protection,
where gravity controls the purest energies;
we are ultimately sheltered by
our very unprotectedness,
and by our turning it towards the Open
when we felt endangered by it,
so that we affirm it in the widest sphere,
wherever the Law affects us.

Beside the sun-drenched street,
in the hollow half tree-trunk,
which long ago became a trough,
a gently self-renewing water-surface,
I slake my thirst, absorbing
the water's gaiety and origin
through my wrists. To drink
would be excessive, too explicit;
but this gesture of deferral lets
bright water fill my consciousness.

So if you came, all I would need
to satisfy myself would be
a gentle laying of my hands
either on your youthful, rounded shoulders,
or on the counterpressure of your breasts.

A bright gift from the cool
mountains
tries to leap into June:
glittering in streams and pools,
renewal pushes on.

Everywhere under dusty
bushes
living water moves,
making its joyful claim
that movement is song.

The space the birds go hurtling through is not
the form-intensifying space you trust.
(Out there, in the open, you deny yourself
and disappear without returning.)

Space reaches out from *us,* translating things.
To realize the being of a tree
project your inner space around it.
Surround it with awareness.
It will not be confined.
Only its reconfiguration
within your emptied mind
can make it fully tree.

As certain things have latent happiness
indestructibly worked into them,
and as a master-actor's slightest move
is freshly woven into permanence;

so, worked as a closely-knit design
into the light fabric of this goatswool shawl
is pure joy, unusable by Nature,
but absorbed into the wonderful

weaving into which life changed itself.
Oh, how much feeling can be saved within
the being and survival of a thing!

Isn't it like breathing, this constant interchange
between attachment and relinquishing,
when something barely *was,* and, vanishing,
is recollected in a nearby face?

World and face: how they displace each other,
and seldom look alike — neither winning . . .
I found the distant slopes fulfilling
yesterday. Today I need not bother

with looking up, or speaking.

Receive a sign from many branches now
as if it were a greeting or reunion;
and, like a bowl for birds to drink from,
let the rain stay mirroring in you.

Nothing is ever lost, it all persists.
Whoever grasps this inwardly can climb
with the top of his ladder leaning
safely against a like-minded world.

Night Sky and Star-Fall

The vast sky, full of glorious restraint,
a wealth of space, an overflow of world.
And we're too distant to configure it,
too near to turn away.

A falling star! Our startled gaze
and our desires closely follow it.
What has begun, and what has disappeared?
What is to blame? And what has been forgiven?

After our long experience, let's risk
another way of saying *House, Tree, Bridge.*
Always addressed to Fate before,
let those words at last speak *out.*

To disentangle the daily life
we each live in our own way,
let's make these symbols we share
constellations in the night.

Gravity

Centre: how you withdraw
from everything, even retrieving yourself
from those who fly: all-powerful centre!

Gravity, like a drink through thirst,
rushes through those who stand.

But falling from those who sleep,
as if from a louring raincloud,
comes a richer downpour of weight.

Waters, plunging and hurrying . . .
brightly uniting, brightly dividing
waters . . . landscape full of motion.
Waters jostling waters,
silences hanging like sounds
above the meadow-slopes.

Is time dissolved in the waters,
which hold back, then hurtle on,
past the forgetful ear?
Meanwhile, from every slope,
does earthly space reach out
into the divine?

Somewhere the flower of parting opens,
dusting us with pollen we inhale,
and even in the just-arriving wind
we breathe departure.

The land is more exposed: homecoming haunts all pathways,
and through the leafless tree appears the enduring house.
Heaven is moving away from us. O heart, now warm the earth,
and make it inwardly ours in this abandoned space.

Earth: give me your best
clay for a vial of tears.
Let my being pour out
the weeping it repressed.

Let everything held back
dissolve in the crafted vessel.
Only Nowhere is bad.
All Existence is right.

Let's leave each other like two stars
divided by the night's excess:
let closeness take the test of distance,
and at the furthest, know itself.

Oh, not to be separate,
not shut out by such a thin screen
from the full measure of the stars.
What is inwardness?
If not intensified sky,
crossed by birds and deep
with homeward winds.

Reluctance to accept the present's gift
without the permission of the future.
We want what's next, even if it's only
space to remember what we have received.

Do you really believe the world is blind
around us? That only we are opposite,
like pockets for the billiard ball?

How much obedience, how many joys
we need to make this task our own:
to let earth sing within the poem,
helping music to emerge from noise.

Or does resistance, rather, make us strong,
and nurture our achievements best?
Does a murderer without a knife love most?
And is life's riskiest undertaking song?

At long last, raised by us denizens, set below the stars,
Window, valid celebration;
you, after lyre and swan, surviving, final,
slowly sanctified picture.

We still need you, gently framed into houses,
Form which promises distances.
Even the lowliest earthly window often
imitates your transfigurations.

Fate has put you down here as its constantly used
measure for loss and transience.
Window out of a steady constellation, emerging,
transformed, beyond what is shown.

Rose, oh pure contradiction, desire to be
no one's sleep under so many
eyelids.

COMMENTARY

Duino Elegies

– The First Elegy: Angels and Lovers

We are terrified by the intensity of beauty represented by the angels. We long for help in our grief, but cannot get it from angels, humans or animals. We fall back on the comfort of habit. Lovers use each other to conceal their solitude. We should share our feelings with Nature; perhaps the birds will pick up something of the emotions we breathe out into the atmosphere. Nature sets us a task: awareness of herself. But we are distracted by the search for personal love. Abandoned lovers, however, like Gaspara Stampa, experience love more intensely and are able to open to the cosmos. We too need to risk abandonment in love, accept it, even welcome it.

Even if we can't bear the voice of God to the extent that saints can, we can still listen to the dead, especially those who died early, and who still need our awareness to help them understand their lives. We divide life from death too sharply; the angels understand that the two interpenetrate and constitute a single realm. Eventually the early dead no longer need us, but we still need the experience of grieving in order to grow spiritually. The Linos myth tells us that music was born from grief at his premature death.

Gaspara Stampa was a young Italian noblewoman born in Padua in 1523. In Venice she fell in love with Count Collaltino. They were happy together for a few years until he left to fight for Henry II in France. On his return he acted coldly towards her, later breaking off with her and marrying another woman. Gaspara Stampa died at age thirty-one after telling the story of the affair in some two hundred sonnets.

The Greek myth of *Linos* exists in several variants. In one he was killed by Apollo for claiming to be as good a musician as Apollo himself. In another, he was Heracles' music teacher, killed by his rebellious student with a blow from a cithara. The general theme of the martyred musician makes this story similar to the Orpheus myth. In both cases, music transcends death.

– The Second Elegy: Angels and Artists

We've lost the easy familiarity with angels we once had; they've become terrifying to us. For example, in the *Book of Tobit* (from the Apocrypha), Tobit sent his son Tobias to fetch money from a distant town. An angel appeared at the door and offered to accompany him on the journey.

However, there are certain symbols or epiphanic experiences which can still give an indirect sense of angelic presence. Angels differ from us in that they gather up again the energy and beauty they have radiated out. We simply lose those moments of intensity. The angels may pick up some of our feelings from these moments, but we cannot. Lovers may touch each other in an attempt to contain and preserve their feelings for each other, but ultimately those feelings still vanish.

Just as we've lost the relationship with the angels we had in biblical times, our art has lost the the capacity which classical Greek sculpture had: to body forth human feeling and contain it aesthetically with grace and calm. Though we may long to, we can no longer find complete emotional satisfaction in our works of art.

In the last part, Rilke seems to echo Hegel's idea that whereas Classical art showed a perfect coinciding of content and form, Romantic Art (meaning in Hegel's terms the art of the Christian era) can only suggest its content through forms that point beyond themselves in some way, just as the soaring Gothic cathedral points away from itself, while the balance of pediment and pillars in the Greek temple perfectly contains its own meaning.

– The Third Elegy: Mothers and Sons

Beneath the personal devotion of lovers lies the primitive, impersonal sex-drive, like a hidden river in the blood. Children are prey to primitive fears of night, and in their dreams may journey back to the origins of human life, including even the sexual act in which they were conceived. The poet shows a young boy making a night-journey towards a primitive origin across a sexualized landscape combining features of natural terrain and the human body. In contrast, the world of security and innocence created by the mother's love and reassurance, and symbolized in the bedroom lamp, seems fragile and limited, though comforting.

– The Fourth Elegy: Fathers and Sons, Angels and Puppets

The trees of our human life (unlike real trees) are not governed by seasonal cycles: thus we do not know when our equivalent of winter is approaching. Further, we humans lack the undivided consciousness of animals, whether the unquestioning strength of the lion or the confident flight of the bird. Divided, we watch our feelings as if they are being acted out on a stage. The poet watches a scene from his own family life, though he would have preferred a puppet show to the unreal pretending of the human actors.

He feels he left a bitter taste of disappointment in his father's mouth. He fears that, even after death, his father is still anxious about him. The poet regrets the shortcomings of his love for others who cared for him and loved him.

Angels could put on a better show with puppets than they can with us, for puppets do not have a divided nature as we do (Rilke alludes here to Heinrich von Kleist's 1810 essay "On the Marionette Theatre.") When we are near death, we can see how much pretence there is in human life, how much we fail to see things as themselves. Children have a more authentic vision, until we hurry them into "growing up" to reassure those who are already "grown-ups." Children do not hide from the idea of death; for them it is quite physical, palpable, like stale bread or an apple core. They fully accept the wholeness of life and death.

"*The boy with squinting brown eyes*" is Rilke's cousin, Egon von Rilke, who died as a child, and is also remembered in *The Sonnets to Orpheus* II, 8.

– The Fifth Elegy: Acrobats

In Munich in the summer of 1915, Rilke stayed in the apartment of friends who owned Picasso's *Les Saltimbanques* (The Acrobats), "the glorious big Picasso beside which I have been living for almost four months now," he wrote. The picture reminded him strongly of Paris (now inaccessible to him because of the Great War), and of the acrobats he had often seen perform there. But the poem does not correspond to the painting in every detail.

The vagrant acrobats symbolize in intensified form the insecure, transient nature of human life. They seem to be serving some relentless Will outside themselves, which treats them in the way Augustus the Strong (1670–1733), Elector of Saxony, used to amuse his guests with feats of physical strength, such as bending tin plates. Yet their group is standing together to form a capital D, as in *Dastehn* (endurance). The group also resembles the centre of a rose, with the audience as the petals, and the dust raised by the performance as the pollen. Yet the amusement of the watchers is shallow, and ultimately they are still bored.

The acrobats create a transient tree with their bodies. The poet senses emotional deprivation under the surface. The unloved boy jumps off the top and smiles tearfully. The girl too is neglected, concealing her nascent sexuality under a public facade.

The poet imagines the acrobatic act failing and disintegrating, but then mysteriously reaching success and perfection. In a parenthetic contrast to this unexpected triumph, Paris is evoked as a showplace for death, personified as a hat maker, Madame Lamort, where social appearance obscures the spiritual meaning of death. Finally a transcendent performance is imagined where the acrobats, now seeming to symbolize all who attempt to love, receive the accolades and coins of the assembled dead.

– The Sixth Elegy: Heroes

The poet takes a natural image for the direct self-realization most humans seem incapable of: the fig-tree's rapid fruition. A second image for this is from myth: Zeus' confident entering of the swan in the story of the rape of Leda. Rilke visited *Karnak* in January 1911 on his journey to Egypt, and saw there the bas-reliefs of the triumphant processions of the pharaoh-generals.

Most humans delay their fruition, distracted by other things. But there are exceptions: heroes and those who die young. Here, the poet focuses on the hero, who faces constantly changing dangers with indifference, always ready to act. The biblical example is *Samson,* whose mother was barren for a long time until she was visited by an angel announcing the birth of a son. Samson's pulling down of the temple was prefigured by his determination to be conceived and by his breaking out of his mother's womb. The hero chooses and controls his destiny, accepting the sacrifices and encouragement of others in pursuing his achievement.

– *The Seventh Elegy: Lovers and Angels*

The poet's voice moves beyond love, beyond the hope of fulfillment through a partner, even though a lover might still be attracted, if not directly sought. Nature would respond to the beginnings of a new theme, beyond wooing; spring would re-echo it as it anticipates the delights of summer dawns, days and starry nights.

More than one lover might be attracted by this ecstatic evocation — the call cannot be limited. Childhood love has an unparalleled intensity, and even in the degraded life of an urban prostitute come moments of complete joy. We should prize happiness even if it doesn't appear to others; it should not need the outward validation of visibility.

Modern culture, through mass-production, is impoverishing the world of material objects. Instead of lasting houses, we have abstract, theoretically conceived units to live in. No temples are being built, and only a few precious traditionally crafted objects survive in our lives, often ignored. Yet we can rebuild this lost richness within our minds, in consciousness. And we can revere the remaining relics of human creativity, like the Sphinx, the temples and the cathedrals.

Yet even these achievements cannot reach the level of the angels. Even a woman in love cannot. We hold up our hand to the angels as if wanting it to be held, but the hand also acts as a shield for ourselves and a warning to the angels to keep their distance — an ambiguous gesture of invitation and fear.

— The Eighth Elegy: Animals and Humans

Human perception and consciousness are compared to those of the animals. The animals look into a space the poet calls *the Open*. It looks like eternity to them, because their death is behind them, unlike humans, for whom time and death are always in front. Humans can only glimpse the Open indirectly, when they see it reflected in an animal's gaze. Children are taught to look at life in the closed, fearful way typical of adults. Only when we near death can we stop looking *towards* it and look out *from* it into the Open.

Lovers sometimes catch a glimpse of the Open behind each other's back, but the other soon blocks this view. We are always *opposite* the created world, never *in* it. We always see the future, whereas animals are unselfconscious, without a separate identity, at one with the whole world.

Yet even animals, at least those born from a womb, feel a melancholy nostalgia for their old home. The world, their second home, is windy and precarious in comparison. Lucky are the animals, like gnats, who are born from exposed seed; for them the whole world is their womb! Womb-born creatures experience a second shock when they have to fly; it seems to break the wholeness of the world like a crack in a cup. Yet the bird exists in both dimensions — womb and world — like *Etruscan souls,* whose bodies were sealed in the tomb, but also represented in a life-size effigy lying on the lid. Humans, in contrast, are always spectators, forming, losing and then re-forming their world, and always saying goodbye to it.

— The Ninth Elegy: Nature and Humans

The poet asks what the point is of being human when we could equally well be a leaf. The answer is that we have a task: even though we are even more transient than the things around us, they need us to complete them with our awareness, just once in each case. We long to take something with us over into the realm of death, but cannot hold on to anything — except perhaps the poetic word that represents the fulfilment of the thing it names. Perhaps Nature invented human love as a way of enjoying her own beauty through the rapturous perceptions of the lovers.

The authenticity of things is diminished in modern technological society, and hence poetic language is even more important. Praise and even grief can be purified into aesthetic objects. Earth's task for us is to transform her visible beauty into invisible beauty, in consciousness and language.

– The Tenth Elegy: The Sorrows

The poet is now able to praise and rejoice *because* of his surrender to tears and sorrow. Our griefs are part of us, our homeland, which can become a place of creative transformation. Yet at present the City of Pain is full of meaningless distractions from grieving. Death is present only in the form of pompous public monuments, the church is closed, and the fairground claims everyone's attention, with its vapid entertainments appealing to greed, violence and lust.

But beyond the advertising placards, a youth wanders off into the landscape of grief, where the Sorrows (female figures representing grief) wait to guide the dead. The youth turns back at first, but is eventually drawn again to travel into a land where grief was once an accepted part of culture and even nature. The youth, with one of the Sorrows as his guide, journeys on into a moonlit night, where they see *the Sphinx*. An owl takes flight from within the rim of the Sphinx's crown, something Rilke had observed on his trip to Egypt in 1911. The sky is full of symbolic constellations, named by the Sorrow. The two pass the spring of joy which flows back down to the human world. The youth continues alone into the mountains

Yet consolation might not always be an uphill struggle. It might simply drop on us, like rain or falling leaves.

The Sonnets To Orpheus

– First Part

(1) Orpheus' song is imaged as a tree surging up and entering the hearer's ear. The uprush of sound immediately rises beyond itself, reaching out and creating silence around itself. This silence is not mere stasis, however. Mysterious new processes are beginning. Orpheus' song is gathering animals from the forest. Though they are still and silent, in contrast to their normal noisiness, this is not an indication of fear or a stratagem. An inner transformation is happening: their hearing is being changed by Orpheus from a mere dark tunnel into a resplendent temple. Creative power is drawn from Nature, is part of Nature, but also transforms Nature. The song acts like a tree, branching into the aural channels of the hearers. The listening animals are moved to a peacefulness beyond their normal natures. They are able to receive more, because the gift of Orphic song transforms their capacity to receive. Art comes from the natural realm, but heightens it, and returns it in this heightened form. The tree and the temple, in the first and last lines, frame the poem with their lofty verticals, contrasting with the low, dark, makeshift dugout which represents the animals' former hearing capacity.

(2) The figure of Wera (who died at age nineteen, and who is commemorated in *The Sonnets*) emanates from the union of Orpheus' lyre and his song, a symbolic parenting for her. (The assumed referent of the initial "it" is Orpheus' song, which then is cited more explicitly as one of the girl's progenitors.) Alternatively, the figure could be seen as representing the "inner feminine" which Rilke felt was present in creators of either sex. The *"springtime veils"* are probably suggested by the diaphanous robes of the female figures in Botticelli's "Primavera," which Rilke had admired in Florence in 1898. The female figure reaches the poet's ear, where she embeds herself or beds down, and goes to sleep. Yet this sleep, like the silence of the

animals, is a transformative space. Within it, Wera's sleep becomes the symbol of all the wonder in the poet's life, wonder at the vivid sensations and feelings derived from trees, fields, and even distant horizons, which seem close enough to be tangible. To say *"she slept the world"* paradoxically has the effect of saying that she woke it up, or re-created it, for her sleep, like her death, has transformative powers. Though she died early, Orpheus, as the spirit of creativity, made Wera perfect within her limited life-span. Her sleep was so fulfilling that she did not need to wake into adulthood. Her death is a gentle fading out, like the natural fading out of Orpheus' own song. Orpheus is familiar with death, both through his visit to the underworld, and through the "dying" of his song. The transience of song represents in heightened form the transience of life, and helps us to accept it.

(3) The divided nature, material and spiritual, of the human mind prevents it from truly following *Apollo,* the god of art. Unlike him, we become caught up in the strings of the lyre, the material dimension of art, while Apollo easily evades this entrapment. We desire to have, rather than simply to be. The poet asks when we might reach a state of pure being, without purposes. When do we exist so purely that we can become the centre of the cosmos? Normally we are too preoccupied with our own desires. Even love, especially in its youthfully ardent form, doesn't truly centre us, because it's still concerned with having, with goals, rather than being. The powerful energy of lovesongs soon runs out. True song (and by implication true art, true existence) is a pure outbreath, without an objective.

(4) Yet love has a value for spiritual progress. If love is a breath, the beloved can enter it, but not detain it. The breath continues after being temporarily divided as it moves past the desired one. The breath is not really meant for the loved one, but for the spiritual progress of the lover who is breathing it out. Requited lovers act both as the bowstring and the target for each other's love-arrows. But unrequited lovers, as Rilke averred in *The First Elegy,* are superior; tearful smiles are "more eternal" than happy ones. The suffering, the heaviness, created by love can be surrendered to the earth, while its lightness merges with the air, blowing across open spaces.

(5) We should not raise a lasting monument to Orpheus, but simply accept his transient commemoration by one rose or another. He is always moving in and out of things. We should be grateful if he lingers a little longer than a bowl of roses. He is present in all singing, but only briefly. We cannot seize him; he has already moved on. Our understanding lags behind him. We grasp what has happened after he has disappeared. His constant transformations may cause him momentary fear, but his nature is to cross boundaries. Like Apollo (I, 3), he doesn't get caught up in the grid of lyre-strings, the instrumentality of art. Transgression, overstepping boundaries, is his form of obedience to his own transformative nature.

(6) This sonnet has a dialogue quality. A question begins it: "Is Orpheus from here?" That is: "Is he a local, a purely earthly being?" The answer is, "No." His nature is broader than that. He grew up in two realms, the upper world of life and the underworld of death. Knowing the willow's roots underground (the underworld) enables him to bend its branches into a lyre; knowledge of death enables him to sing of life. Further, in some versions of the myth, Orpheus took a willow bough down to Hades with him as a talisman.

Instructions are given, according to traditional "superstitious" beliefs, not to leave food out overnight. It will attract the dead. However, they should not be shunned: a better way of being aware of them is to let Orpheus conjure them up and make them an element in the whole of visual experience, so that their ghosts blend in with everything seen. Traditional practices like spells which involve burning plants are as meaningful to Orpheus as clear scientific cause-and-effect relationships. Humble household objects, or common ornaments, like the jug, clasp and ring are valid symbols for Orpheus. These examples might be found in daily use domestically, or buried with the dead, the latter being a common practice of traditional cultures, showing a wise intimacy with the kingdom of death which has been lost in modernity. This interconnecting of life-world and death-world corresponds to Orpheus' own nature.

(7) Orpheus' task is to praise; this is what he is summoned to do. Praise is unlike the wooing lovesongs treated earlier, in that it expresses being rather than desiring or having. The praise-giving

Orpheus is like precious ore running out of rock-formations, or like a transient wine-press creating endless wine for us. He transforms the landscape into a warm, passionate, southerly vineyard. The existence of death and its associations (shadow, decay, crypt) does not invalidate his praise. He is like a messenger bringing fruit into the world of the dead, reaching out to offer it to them far behind the door of their kingdom, for them to praise, if not eat. The idea of providing food for the dead resembles the burial practices mentioned in the previous sonnet, where the dead are provided with useful objects for the next world.

(8) Sorrow and Praise might seem incompatible at first sight, but for Orpheus they belong together like spiritual sisters. *"The nymph of the weeping well"* is Byblis, who hunted so passionately for her lost lover that she finally died from exhaustion; a hurrying stream appeared in her place (Ovid, *Metamorphoses,* IX). Sorrow purifies and sanctifies our outpouring of tears, until the stream can approach the realm of the sacred, symbolized by the portals and altars. Sorrow goes on learning after her sisters have finished: Joy knows things quickly, and Longing is soon assuaged. But Sorrow goes on working on old wounds, until she is able to project, however tentatively and awkwardly, a constellation of our grieving voices into the sky. Grief is lifted heavenwards, transformed into a link between the stars. The constellation is an important recurring symbol for Rilke of how human imagination creates a design out of the given phenomena of nature like the stars, in which different cultures see different images. The Plough, the Big Dipper, and the rest are projections of human meaning onto a cosmic scale.

(9) Sorrow's lifting of grief skywards is echoed by Orpheus' lifting the lyre in the underworld. The acceptance of grief and death is the essential prelude to true praise. Only after he has eaten the poppy of oblivion with the dead, will the singer's notes be able to last. Paradoxically, acceptance of loss leads to permanence. We can still know the image inwardly, even if its outer reflection dissolves. Voices last, not by clinging to life, but by inhabiting the double realm of life-and-death together, eternal and mild, unlike the lover's passionate outburst which soon fades away (I, 3).

(10) The poet takes new symbols of the togetherness of life and death: the old tombs or sarcophagi in Rome which have been converted into drinking troughs for animals, and the tombs in the fields of Arles, in France, now lidless and open, occupied by plants and butterflies. The sealed death-chamber finds a new life-use. These formerly closed tombs are now like re-opened mouths, which have known silence, the precondition of speech or song. The poet asks us, as friends, whether or not we have learned the meaning of silence. Both knowing silence and ignorance of silence are marked on the human face. Our faces show evidence of authentic and inauthentic self-expression, respectively grounded and ungrounded in silence.

(11) Humans, with their pride of earth, project their own ideas into the sky by patterning the stars into constellations. One example of such a "star-picture" might be an image of the togetherness of horse and rider, animal and human. But this conjunction might be only a temporary unity. After all, on Earth, horse and rider separate when the ride is over and it is time to eat: one goes to a pasture, the other to a table. Strictly speaking, the constellation is an illusion, but one that is nevertheless good for us to believe in as a figure, as a symbol. These provisional self-projections onto the universe are enough to satisfy us temporarily.

(12) This sonnet's argument follows on directly from that of the preceding one. Symbolic designs like constellations are vital to us even if they are illusory. They help us to live more truly, and unite us more authentically than the clock time that co-ordinates our activities. Although we are often not grounded in our true existence, we sense it as if by antennae, and receive an answering music of natural forces. These potentially disturbing intimations are masked by the busy daily life we lead. We try to control Nature, like the farmer planning and worrying about the crops which mean survival to him. But ultimately we cannot penetrate Nature's secret. The creative transformation of seed into summer is not accessible to our ordinary understanding. We do not extract the bounty of Nature. Rather, Nature gives to us of its own accord.

(13) Fruit is one of Nature's gifts. The act of eating fruit brings the togetherness of life and death into our mouths. Children's sense of

wonder at this experience (which may be too familiar for adults) can be seen in their faces. The poet attempts to express this in words, even though the "discoveries" flowing from the fruit pulp take the place of words in the mouth at first. Eating an apple is an everyday experience, but it becomes strange and wonderful if we really pay attention to it, like a child. The experience of tasting fruit could literally take the words out of our mouths, silence us with astonishment. Yet in the last five lines the poet does take up the challenge of describing this indescribable feeling after it is over. The sweetness is condensed, then intensified, and finally clarified in its meaning. Like Orpheus' music, it points in both directions, and has a double meaning ("ambiguous"); it links life and death, sun and earth, the distant and the local. The small everyday action of eating an apple has become immense; it has expanded to focus and unite the cosmos.

(14) Fruit, flowers and leaves are all natural forms which mediate between the dark earth and the open air. These two dimensions also connote the realms of the dead and of the living. The significance of the fruit, flowers and leaves, the "language" they speak to us, is not merely seasonal, a way of marking the phases of the year. These colourful forms are out in the open, bright and obvious. But they may also conceal something behind these conspicuous statements, the poet speculates. Does the brightness carry a glint of envy from the dead, who nourish and fertilize the earth? Are the dead the slaves of the living, resentfully doing our bidding, as we seek to master and organize the earth's fertility? Or is it the other way around, with the dead as the masters, giving us freely the gifts which we think we have produced (as "produce") by ourselves? As in the previous sonnet, fruits are seen as links, hybrid forms like Orpheus himself, uniting death and life, strength and love.

(15) The taste of the fruit is soon gone. We cannot hold on to a taste any more than we can any other experience. But once it has gone, it can be celebrated through creative response. We can re-live it through artistic recreation or re-creation. The poet invites girls to "dance the orange," reinterpreting the taste through physical movement. The fruit has become part of those who have eaten it, so now

they can project a suitable landscape for it through their warm and uninhibited dancing.

(16) The dog, addressed as "my friend," inhabits a world marked out by human signs and interpretations, a world in which the dog is isolated because these are not meanings it has created. The dog inhabits the world of smell, yet can intuitively sense many of our emotions, such as our fear of the dead. It is difficult for humans and dogs to reach a common, holistic understanding of the world they share. The poet warns the dog against too exclusive a devotion to the human world, against too great a domination by its master. But the dog, like Esau, may be the true (though unintended) inheritor of the world. The poet will guide the hand of *his* master (Orpheus) onto the dog's skin, just as Isaac's hand was guided onto the arm of Jacob, his younger, smooth-skinned son. But Jacob's arm was covered in an animal pelt so that Isaac would mistake it for Esau's, the older, hairy-skinned son's. Jacob received the blessing intended for Esau, and the dog rather than the human may receive Orpheus' blessing.

(17) The poet evokes the great tree of human cultural development from the hidden, tangled, confused roots of prehistory, through the era of hunting and war, leavened by the wisdom of the old and the peace and beauty of women, until out of the struggles among the branches, a single one emerges and curves into a lyre, symbolizing the emergence of song and poetry at the crown of cultural progress. The poem could also refer to Rilke's own family tree (which he believed to be aristocratic), with himself, the poet, as its highest issue.

(18) The poet hails his master Orpheus from the din of the machine age, where technology and its champions demand praise. Yet the machine is weakening us, unless we keep it firmly in place as a servant, not a master, for us. We gave it our strength, but should not give it our love.

(19) Although change on earth seems endless, there is a centre or home for anything that has completed its journey. Orpheus' song endures beyond passing and change (even though, as the poet states

elsewhere, it endures precisely *by* its changing nature). We exist incompletely, without full knowledge of love, grief, or death; yet we can still be blessed and healed by Orphic song.

(20) The poet wishes to offer his master, Orpheus, a gift appropriate to his role as a teacher of hearing. He chooses a memory of a horse he saw in Russia. The horse's fettered leg cannot prevent the soaring joy of its galloping in the fields, just as suffering in human life need not impede, and may even enhance, our creativity. Orpheus' myth is complete in this one example, just as the horse is healed, or made whole, by entering the circle of that myth. The poem is based on Rilke's visit to Russia with Lou Andreas-Salomé in 1900. He recounts the return of this memory in a letter to Lou of 11 February 1922.

(21) Spring returns with childlike joy, reciting the poetry it has learned under the strict tutelage of Winter, a poetry which can name afresh the blue and green around it. Earth is playing games like a child; the "roots" and "stems" that are common to language and nature have been thoroughly learned and can now be effortlessly sung out.

(22) Movement and stillness are balanced against each other. Humans have a will or drive to achieve, to progress. Yet this happens within time, which is insignificant within eternity. Our urgency is temporary, and our first sense of the sacred was of something enduring. Thus boyish obsessions with speed and flight need to give way to a sense of stillness, where dark and light, nature and culture (flower and book) have found a balance.

(23) Flying can only become spiritual when it transcends boyish glee in technological prowess and becomes pure exploration and discovery. The solo-pilot nearing the horizon is inwardly united with his destination.

(24) We have lost contact with the gods. Should we forget about them or try to find where they are on a map (the symbol of scientifically organized space). Our industries, our machines, have no connection to the divine. Once bathing was a sacred ritual, as was feasting; but now both are merely secular. Our world has speeded up so that

we lack the patience to wait for messages from the gods. Our world, without the divine, has become oriented only towards the human. But increased human interdependence has not brought us closer together. On the contrary, we are lonelier now, and know even less about each other than we did before. In a purely utilitarian way, we build straight roads rather than winding, meandering ways. All of our fire is spent in huge industrial steam-boilers to drive larger and larger machines, where formerly fire was an agent of sacrificial ritual. Like exhausted swimmers, we are losing our inner strength, sapped by the technology we have created.

(25) The poet evokes Wera again through his image of her at play, although she is terribly close to the cry of anguish expressing her disease and death. She is seen as a dancer, frozen into stillness like a sculpture. While her companions continue to dance, she can only listen to the music. She recovers from the illness briefly, like a stream emerging from the shadows, only to relapse and enter the open gate of death.

(26) In contrast, Orpheus continued to sing even after his death at the hands of the crazed Maenads, the female followers of Dionysus, whom he is said to have scorned after turning away from love of women when he lost Eurydice a second time. His head and lyre survived the attack intact, the stones being mysteriously softened and repelled before striking him. Eventually, though, he was dismembered. Yet even this had the effect of only extending and scattering his music. It lingers on in nature and in humans, who are now able to be mouths of Nature as well as hearers of Orpheus.

– *Second Part*

(1) Breathing and poetry are both interchanges between inner and outer worlds. Breath creates a rhythm within which the self seems to occur as a mere incident. Or the self is a sea crossed by a single wave that represents the present moment's breath. The sea of the self is ecologically thrifty, constantly recycling space as breath recycles air. The air is full of pockets once breathed in and out by the poet. It is

familiar, like a family member. The air, through breath, makes possible the poet's words, just as the rind and leaf make possible the fruit.

(2) Experiences are not lost, only recycled. This theme is the same as that of the previous sonnet, and the whole of the second cycle of sonnets is a recycling of the themes of the first cycle. The material vehicle of expression is less important than the expression itself, like a brilliant sketch made on a piece of scrap paper. A mirror-reflection might catch the essence of a girl's facial expression when she is alone one morning, while other, more flattering, lighting might disguise her real face. Paradoxically, the mirror reflection has more authenticity than the real face, which may simply be the reflection of that reflection. Many longings have been expressed only by staring into a fire and fantasizing. They are lost, like so much else in life. Despite all this loss, Orpheus still praises the heart from which these longings come. Loss is reborn or recycled within the total process of life-and-death that the poet calls the All.

(3) Continuing the inquiry of the previous sonnet, the poet states that the mysterious importance of mirrors has not been fully understood. By seeming to swallow momentary images of humans, they create gaps in time. They are themselves full of holes. They create a walled-off space that is nevertheless penetrable by certain significant images. Not everyone is admitted, but the greatest beauty is retained until Narcissus is released into the mirror-space.

(4) Love is able to produce mythic creatures like the unicorn, a traditional symbol of virginity in the Middle Ages. Love enables non-existent creatures like this to *become* by leaving room for the imaginary being to realize itself, nourished only on possibility, not the mundane actuality of food. The unicorn's horn is an outgrowth of this sense of the possible. It attains a kind of imaginative being in the silver mirror (metal mirrors were common in the Middle Ages) and in the eyes of the virgin who beholds the unicorn there.

(5) Flowers are the theme of the next three sonnets. The poet imagines the anemone being controlled by a muscle, which opens it to receive the light in the morning, and gathers back the petals in the

evening. Humans are more violent and more enduring, but rarely as open and receiving as this flower.

(6) Rilke speculated that the wild eglantine was the rose of ancient Persia, its few petals contrasting with the modern, many-petalled rose. Both are celebrated here, the richly layered and the relatively unclothed types. The rose echoes through the history of poetry, and is still vividly present, as well as evoking personal and cultural memories.

(7) In this sonnet, a single complex sentence links and reconciles the flowers with the female hands which cut and arrange them. The cut flowers receive resuscitation from the water in the vases, and are able to heal by shedding the warmth of the girls' hands in the fresh coolness. Ultimately these girls are relatives of the flowers: they heal as well as wound them.

(8) This sonnet is dedicated to Rilke's cousin Egon von Rilke (1873–1880). The poet invokes the small group of his childhood playmates, who often communicated in silence, like the lamb in medieval paintings whose words are inscribed on a scroll extending from its mouth. Moments of happiness while the children were playing seemed free, not owned or due to anyone in particular, though dissipating into the surrounding space and the subsequent time, filled with childhood anxieties. The moments seem to be unknown by others; the surrounding passers-by, traffic and houses are oblivious. Even the children themselves are not real. The only reality there is apparently the arc of the ball through the air. But one child, Egon, steps into reality as he places himself under the falling ball. The arc of the ball creates a configuration which, like a constellation in relation to the stars it unites, is more real than what it configures.

(9) Justice has become more humane since the days of the neck-iron for holding delinquents and the rack for torturing heretics in the Middle Ages. But these reforms have not really come from the heart. The death penalty has only been given up reluctantly. True mercy would be more powerful and radiant, and would reach out beyond those who are already well protected. True mercy comes quietly from within.

(10) Technology should stay out of the spiritual realm and obey human ends, rather than have humans serve it. It has already displaced traditional handicrafts with its harsh treatment of materials such as stone, and its mechanically produced buildings. It dominates life instead of remaining confined to the factory. Nevertheless, our sense of the magical nature of existence still springs up repeatedly. Language cannot fully express it, but music can still create sacred structures, not in stone like the machine, but in vibrations that reach beyond utilitarian ends.

(11) In October 1911, while beginning his winter sojourn in Duino Castle, Rilke visited the Karst, the limestone hills nearby, to see a pigeon hunt. The birds were decoyed out of the caves by a canvas strip dangled into the entrance and then twitched. The poet asserts that this way of administering death should not evoke pity, since it is only an example of the many ways humans have traditionally hunted animals. Killing is part of the sorrow of the human journey, and whatever happens to us on that journey should be accepted with serenity.

(12) Transformation should be accepted and even willed. Shapes are changed as if within a flame, and the moment of change is the most precious one. Beings which are intent solely on survival become rigid and try to become inconspicuously grey. Yet this hardness only evokes something even harder, which will smash it. Better to flow like water, accepting and enjoying the rhythmic identity of beginnings and endings. Beauty is created by separating, not clinging. Daphne, who was changed into a laurel tree to escape the pursuit of Apollo (a story told by Ovid, *Metamorphoses*, I), urges the reader to undergo a metamorphosis into wind.

(13) Separation should be anticipated, not avoided. You have to survive it, like winter. The death of Eurydice, and Orpheus' own death, have to be accepted, affirmed and even praised. Destruction should not be shunned but experienced intensely, like a glass shattering as it gives out its ringing sound. Being and non-being together constitute the ground of the perfect inner vibration, which only needs to occur once. When Orpheus adds himself to the infinite totality of nature, it completes and at the same times annihilates the total (one).

(14) We project our own Fate, our own feelings, onto flowers. But perhaps we should reverse this, and feel those imputed feelings (if they exist) ourselves, on behalf of the flowers. Nature is full of willing changes, but humans are more ponderous, tiring nature out with our imposed teachings. We should let things transform us by yielding to them as if to sleep. Or we might be accepted by them and become one of them, fully exposed to nature.

(15) The fountain is like a mouth for a "flow" of speech, a mask for the liquid face of the water. The fountain's supply of water (speech) is carried from distant mountains, past graves (death), to be received by the basin (ear). Earth is speaking to herself from this mouth (fountain) to this ear (basin). A jug (human intervention) would cause a break in this circuit of self-communication.

(16) Just as we interrupt nature's colloquy with herself, so we tear up what Orpheus heals. This process is analogous to the tearing up of Orpheus himself by the Maenads, and his subsequent distribution throughout nature. The cutting edge is our scientific curiosity, whereas Orpheus is diffused serenely everywhere. The next verse is a recollection of Rilke's journey in Egypt in 1911, where he saw a relief of the gods standing opposite the gifts freely offered up by the devotees. We are kept at a distance from the source of knowledge: we can hear the spring, but the dead are able to drink from it as well. The lamb, humbler than we are, desires his bell, accepting his limitation to the realm of sound.

(17) Humans look for the fruits of comfort in gardens, in trees, among blossoms, but they might be found also amidst the field of our own suffering. The fruit seem to survive whole, unspoiled by pecking birds or burrowing worms. Perhaps these fruits are free gifts, from trees not owned and cultivated by us, but by angels working slowly and secretly. Humans tend to ripen and rot more quickly than these fruits, but this fact does not disturb the calm summers that produced their equanimity.

(18) Wera is evoked in a triple transformation, where a spinning dancer turns into a tree, the tree turns into a vase, and the vase ripens like a fruit. The dancer achieves the feat of transposing transience into motion, that is, intensifying itself. The tree, like the girls

who "dance the orange" (in I, 13), projects an entire climate and environment from itself. But it also bears more solid fruit. The vase formed on the spinning wheel of the dance bears the trace of the spinning eyebrows of the dancer as part of its painted decorations.

(19) Two contrasted spaces are defined in the modern city. One is the space of money: the banks with their deferential service, the shops retailing the marks of wealth, such as silk and fur garments. The second is that of indigence, shunned instinctively by money, so that even a copper penny treats a beggar's hand as a void. It feels that it has been taken out of circulation, as if it had rolled into a dusty corner under the wardrobe in a bedroom. Money never stops breathing: it is operating twenty-four hours a day. But paradoxically the beggar stands in the pause of this incessant breathing. The open hand endures day after day (though closed at night like the anemone of II, 6) as a symbol of human vulnerability, celebrated only by the poet and by Orpheus.

(20) The distance between humans can actually be greater than the immense distances between the stars. This applies even to children or to women in love when they both desire and avoid the men who love them. Our Fate is to be alienated from Being, distant from other beings, unable to communicate. Even something as domestic as a plate of fish on the dinner table can seem unutterably mysterious if we look more closely at the fish's face. Fish cannot speak, but perhaps through imagination we can speak in their place, and articulate what they might have said.

(21) Imagination is further celebrated as the poet invites his heart to praise gardens only heard of but never seen, like those in Persia. The heart in imagination dwells with the branches, blossoms and fruits of the fabled gardens, mixed into the air. Nothing has to be renounced in the fullness of existence: the silk thread of imagination is always part of the woven fabric of life. Even if we feel the design of our (Persian) carpet is dominated by misery, the silk thread is always part of the whole.

(22) In spite of Fate (by which Rilke means the outward constraints of the human condition), human creativity has expressed itself in parks, statues, arches, balconies, bells and the single column he saw

in Karnak in Egypt. Unfortunately this creativity is now being wasted on technological projects such as racing cars and aeroplanes, whose frenzy of speed leaves nothing behind like the architectural heritage mentioned previously. Yet perhaps the pursuit of speed is not a complete waste after all. These flights leave no trace, but human thought may not do so either.

(23) Orpheus offers to help us understand those moments whose meaning is most elusive. These moments are most truly our own, just as those which seemed to welcome us initially, eventually reject us and our interpretations. We always seek to get a grip on experience, but often fail because we are too young to accept the old or traditional meanings, and too old and traditional to imagine the nonexistent. We should refuse the security of known and familiar meanings, and accept danger as if it ripened and sweetened like a fruit.

(24) The ground-breaking urge of humanity is irrepressible. Explorers set off with little backing, yet new settlements arose and prospered. We create the gods through our projections, though both can be destroyed by Fate or human limitation. But despite that, they are immortal. They will outlast us, so we should listen to the god (Orpheus) who will eventually listen to *us*. The unity of the human endeavour over millennia is created by parents nurturing the future through children who will supplant and replace them. Our adventures may be ventures on the part of Death, who speculates on our lives in order to make a profit.

(25) The ground-breaking theme continues with the sound of the first ploughs of Spring. Human rhythm has been absent over the Winter from the earth, which is tense with anticipation of the spring. Even though Spring has come many times before, it never loses its novelty. We can't grasp it, because it grasps us first. Even in the midst of Winter there are signs of future Spring in the brown leaves that have hung on and in the black of bushes and dung-heaps. Time seems to be going backwards towards youth.

(26) Rilke's late poetry observes a distinction between crying out (as at the beginning of *The First Elegy*) and singing. Sonnet I, 3 also moves from the vocal outburst of the youth in love to the "different

breath" with which true Orphic song is created. Here, the cries of birds and children are heard as striking and disturbing, as breaks in the fabric of reality, gaps in the ordered world we are accustomed to, wedges driven into outward normality. Dreams are similar challenges to habitual perceptions. Cries are still part of Fate (human limitation) or perhaps protests against it, or expressions of it. As such, the cries are scattered in the air like loose kites. Only Orphic song can gather them up and make them into a harmony, a vehicle to sustain those cries as the stream sustained Orpheus' head and lyre after his dismemberment by the Maenads.

(27) The poet wonders aloud if the much-discussed destructiveness of time is a reality. The castle on the hill looks enduring and secure. Can the Demiurge (the mythic Greek deity who made the world) really destroy the poet's heart? Perhaps we are not so weak as Fate (human limitation) wants us to feel, and perhaps it is not so hard to fulfill our childhood promise. If we simply accept what life offers, transience, far from being a destroyer, will become a ghost and pass through us like smoke. Even so, we need not be merely passive. Our active striving for achievement is also divine in its way.

(28) Coming and going is the basic Orphic rhythm, alternating sound and silence, life and death. Wera the dancer is invoked again to elevate her dance's overall pattern into a constellation; both symbolize the human capacity to unify and hence imaginatively surpass the ordinary round of nature. Nature herself needs arousing by the human creativity Orpheus represents. Wera feels Nature is somewhat tardy in receiving the Orphic message and responding to it. She still resonates inwardly to the "centre," the centring place which focuses and concentrates the diffuse life of Nature, the centre where his lyre sounded at the beginning of the first part (in I, 1). Wera's purpose in learning to dance was to inspire the poet, her friend, to turn towards Orphic celebration.

(29) The friend could be the poet, as in the preceding sonnet, now receiving the Orphic teaching through Wera. Or the "you" could be Orpheus himself, hearing his teaching repeated by the poet-adept. Either makes sense, given the interchangeability of the various roles in the cycle. Breath and space are united: breath creates space. Just

as breath comes from the lungs, so the bright sounds of bells emerge from dark belfries. The self is no longer self-contained, but is in symbiosis with its environment; as the self is consumed, it nourishes its surroundings, and is thus transformed into them. Transformation means changing places, reversal. The bitter taste of bad experiences can be transformed by becoming the wine. The senses reach their limits in the immense night of Orphic transformation — they cross or contradict each other, but meaning can still emerge from this situation. Human speech, the site of transformation, makes a complementary/contradictory response to its surroundings, Nature. Confronted with the motionless earth, humanity asserts its movement, its transience, its flow of consciousness. Confronted with the transience of Nature, as in the flowing stream, humanity asserts its own stillness in existence, with an "I am" reminiscent of Descartes' very different cogito, "I think, therefore I am." Rilke's cogito is a twofold reply to Nature.

The Last Poems

We've listened . . . This sonnet was written between 17 and 19 February 1922 at Muzot, and was probably originally intended for *The Sonnets to Orpheus*. The poet elaborates a series of paradoxes around the flow of a fountain: always changing yet always the same, temporal yet eternal, apart yet part of oneself, local yet exotic, remote yet closely related, clear yet mysterious, insignificant yet significant. When we respond emotionally to objects, we don't know how they receive our feeling or where they take it.

That nothing . . . Written before Christmas 1923. Loss is a form of possession: we come to own our experiences, not by clinging to them, but by relinquishing them. The totality of the universe is such that even actions intended to be destructive are self-defeating because they bring about new creations by clearing the space for them.

Silence. Written on 23 January 1924 in a copy of *Duino Elegies* as a dedication to Frau Fanette Clavel, whom Rilke had met in Basel in 1919. The poet expresses his idea of true poetic speech. True silence is not simply a gap in the endless superficial chatter that fills our minds and our media. Authentic silence nurtures the roots of authentic speech. When words emerge from this deeper inner tranquillity, they overcome the malign effects of the prattle that continues even within superficial outward silence. However, we cannot retain or possess these authentic utterances except, paradoxically, by surrendering them completely to the world.

Give your heart a sign . . . Written in February 1924 at Muzot. When humans cling to emotional suffering, they can immure themselves in a fixed feeling of doom, burden, incarceration. Release can come through acknowledging natural shifts like a change of wind, or through being aware of divine presences. If we can recognize the immense web of connections that relate us to other beings, the sense of rigid isolation can soften and melt away.

Even our losses . . . Written on 7 February 1924 as a dedication in a copy of *Duino Elegies* for Hans Carossa, a doctor and poet Rilke had met in Munich. The "we" or "us" refers in the first instance to poets, but by extension applies to all who live poetically. We remain related to everything we have lost or forgotten. In fact this losing and forgetting is a condition of true ownership of one's experience. We surrender it to transformation, but something remains constant in this process, perhaps just a shape. Experiences are continually recycled around us. Even though we are not often at the centre of this cycle or circle, we are always within its scope. The circle is a sacred form, symbol of unbroken continuity.

A blackbird . . . Written in mid-February 1924 at Muzot. This poems juxtaposes two birds and two seasons. In late Autumn the blackbird's note sounds retrospective, looking back at the past in the way a later note recalls or mirrors an earlier note in musical composition. In early Spring (February was usually a creative month for Rilke), a finch's note has an anticipatory sound, heralding a bolder venture than memory, one that is in keeping with the opening possibilities of the new year.

Early Spring. Written on 20 February 1924 at Muzot. Rilke always treasured the first intimations of Spring in late Winter, when slight changes of colour, sound and feeling give the first premonitions of Winter relenting. Paths seem to lead "to it," referring presumably to the "early Spring" of the title. The bare trees seem to fill with foreshadowing of summer foliage. These very delicate changes show Rilke's idea that the first inklings of a process contain (virtually) the whole process.

Transience. Written in late February 1924 at Muzot. The first quatrain appears to be largely a traditional lament for transience, imaged in the decay and ruin of human edifices. But the second quatrain moves to question this — why should this process be lamented any more than the fall of water back into a fountain basin? We should persist in the face of change (while not resisting it), which will in some way recognize our persistence, even while it appears to be destroying our intentions and achievements.

Already sap . . . Written in early March 1924, this poem continues the early Spring theme. In Winter, natural life takes refuge underground in the roots. The poet shows the moment when this deep inner life is reviving, but has not yet manifested itself. The future is still unnoticed, still protected, but is intuited by birds, bushes, and trees.

Walk. This poem of early March 1924 concerns our "dialogue," or interchange with Nature. We look ahead down a road, say, to a hill, which seems to recognize us before we can recognize it. The experience of the numinous (epiphany) seems to reach us from outside. It changes us, but only to make us more true to our inner selves, of which we are normally unconscious. In sum, we give a sign to Nature, and Nature gives us a countersign. But we may not fully understand this response, except perhaps as some movement towards us, like a headwind.

Streams enrapture the land . . . This poem of early May 1924 shows the Spring drunkenly staggering around in the new greenery, and breathing through the flowers, while the nightingales hold an all-day practice for outdoing the stars at night.

Joy, restrained . . . Written in mid-May 1924, inspired by the transition to two days of sunshine after a period of heavy rains at Muzot. The release of happiness follows restraint. Summer is felt to be present within the Spring weather. The blossoms are over and Summer foliage is beginning to appear. Each tree seems to have its own envelope of space around it. Each day seems full of the next day: the future is virtually present now.

Do you still remember . . . Written on 1 June 1924, this poem concerns our resistance to responding fully to the powerful manifestations of Nature. The falling stars are like horses galloping across the sky, but we set up fences in a vain effort to restrain their flight. The rash, daring playfulness of the shooting stars, however, can heal our timorous hearts if we can endure the spectacle.

Just as Nature . . . Written on 6 June 1924 as a dedication poem to Helmuth Freiherr Lucius von Stoedtner, then German Ambassador at the Hague, in a copy of Rilke's novel *The Notebooks of Malte Laurids Brigge* (1910). This powerful and mysterious philosophical poem is discussed at length in Martin Heidegger's essay "What are Poets For?" Life consists of risk. The existence of every plant and animal is an act of daring, since Nature does not safeguard these beings. Human life as well is risked by the Ground of our being. But we are more conscious of this than other beings, and can choose to assent to the risk or even increase the stakes. In fact, we find a new safety in stepping beyond self-protection. When menaced by feelings of insecurity, we can surrender them to the Open, Rilke's term for the world as we experience it when we are not separated from it by ego. We can affirm our unprotectedness, our acceptance of the risk of existence, whenever we are touched by the universe. What did Rilke mean by the Law *(das Gesetz)* of the last line? Perhaps something akin to the Hindu and Buddhist term "Dharma," which has a range of meanings including the truth, the way things are, the laws of Nature and the laws by which we should live.

Beside the sun-drenched street . . . Written in early June 1924 at Muzot. The poet satisfies his thirst, not by drinking, but by letting the cool water run over his wrists. In the same way, his desire for his lover can be satisfied by a touch. The satisfaction of desire does not have to be literal; it can be stilled by a lighter contact. This restraint, or lightness of touch, in approaching experience, is characteristic of late Rilke. Less can be more; a taste can be more intense than a meal. We do not have to "have" things; we may appreciate them better in gentler, non-possessive ways.

A bright gift . . . Written on 16 June 1924 at Muzot. The movement of fresh mountain water across a dusty landscape is a metaphor for the action of poetry. The poem's last line recalls the claim that "Song is Being" from *The Sonnets to Orpheus* I, 3.

The space . . . Written on 16 June 1924 at Muzot. The space the birds move through in flight is an exterior space, not constituted in the same way as the inner space we inhabit and create through our perception. This inner space intensifies forms (the poem takes the example of a tree) by surrounding them with our awareness, and thereby *realizing* them both subjectively (becoming conscious of them) and objectively (making them real). Paradoxically, by projecting our own inner space in this manner, we receive it back enriched, whereas if we treat exterior space as something apart from us, we simply lose ourselves in it.

As certain things have latent happiness . . . Written on 1 July 1924 in Ragaz, shortly after Rilke's visit to Henri Moser's collection of cashmere shawls in the Historical Museum in Bern, Switzerland. The patient handiwork that goes into the weaving of a shawl becomes a symbol of how human subjectivity can become embodied in a "thing," a word which has an intimate and positive resonance for Rilke (as opposed to the negative quality of "object"). The weaving work is as creative as the gesture of a master-actor, which the poet takes paradoxically as the symbol of permanence. The transient gesture still becomes part of the "texture" (weaving) of the fabric of life. The true artifact can become a repository of human feelings of joy and happiness.

Isn't it like breathing . . . Written in mid-July 1924 in Ragaz. The theme is again the reciprocity between self and world, an interchange that should be as natural as breathing. If we do not cling to the joys that come our way, and let them dissolve instead, we may see them recreated in the face of another person. There is a constant exchange between the world and the human face as it expresses responses; the two do not match exactly (this is a process of transformation) and neither dominates the relationship. Human feeling may find expression in a landscape, so that it may not need a further outlet for a while.

Receive a sign . . . Written in mid-July 1924 in Ragaz. It is possible to have a personal relationship with Nature, so that branches, for example, can seem to offer greetings. Humans can become receptive or reflective vessels, holding the rain like a bird-bowl. Nature is a totality where nothing is ever lost, only transformed or recycled. Nature balances the human ascent to greater understanding by supporting it in the way a ladder is supported by what it leans against.

Night Sky and Star-Fall. Written in mid-August 1924 in Ragaz. The idea of Fall has mostly negative connotations in Western culture (e.g., the Fall of Man, a fallen woman). But Rilke wanted often to give a positive sense to falling, as in the last lines of *The Tenth Elegy.* On 20 December 1919 he wrote to Nanny Wunderly-Volkart, "there is no *below* in sacred space." Falling stars held a special significance for him. Here, the night sky is seen as limitless, overflowing, and yet still ordered, in a way we cannot fully map or configure, but equally cannot ignore. A falling star has significance for us, though we may not be able to determine what that is.

After our long experience . . . Written in August 1924 in Muzot. Common words describing human experience (house, tree, bridge, and so on) are usually addressed to Fate, Rilke's term for the factors which limit and determine human life. But now (perhaps poetically) we can direct those words elsewhere, outwards into the unlimited, where they can take on their full power, like constellations in the night sky. We live daily life and use language in a prosaic way to refer to our particular circumstances, our house, etc. But the poetic word uttered outwards without these local limitations can unite humanity across differences, and make us more at home in the universe.

Gravity. Written on 5 October 1924 at Muzot. Gravity as a universal force provides a symbol of the coherence of the world, which includes three human ways of relating to the ground: flying (compare *The Sonnets to Orpheus* I, 23), standing upright, and lying down. Gravity is seen here as an energy (like *chi* in the Asian understanding) which moves intimately *through* these three modes of being, rather than merely operating on them neutrally as an outside force.

Waters, plunging and hurrying . . . Written in mid-October 1924 at Muzot. Time and space in these last poems are not neutral, measurable universals which *contain* events and things, but rather are intimately *involved* with them. Time can be dissolved, and space created, by the action of things and events in the world. Here the waters rushing down a valley between high meadow-slopes disturb the normal sense of hearing by their intermittencies of sound and silence. Our usual time-sense is likewise disoriented, and the slopes seem to create space from themselves, space in which the earthly and divine realms are united. A poetic experience like this reconfigures around itself what we usually think of as separate, neutral dimensions.

Somewhere the flower of parting . . . Written at Muzot in mid-October 1924. Parting is latent in every experience of connection, but parting can itself be seen as a flower whose pollen we continually inhale, breathing in the seeds of new experiences. Even something that has just begun contains its own departure latent within it.

The land is more exposed . . . Written in late October 1924. Autumn exposes the landscape and all beings seek refuge for the Winter. Modernity has distanced the gods from us (see *The Sonnets to Orpheus* I, 24), but our emotions can reclaim some of the space they have recently abandoned.

Earth: give me . . . Written on 30 October 1924 at Muzot. Rilke writes in *The Tenth Elegy* that "we waste our sorrows." This poem offers a way of treasuring them. It describes a lachrymatory, or tear-bottle. This is a small phial or vial found in Roman tombs. This tiny clay vessel links the earth it is made from with the water (tears) it holds. Instead of being contained (repressed) within the inhibited body, the tears can be contained in the artifact (the tear-vial is a symbol of the poem and the art-work in general). All actual existence, including grief, is ultimately right, appropriate, justified; only an emotional Nowhere is bad.

Let us leave each other like two stars . . . Written in early summer 1925 in Paris. Once again the poet takes up the theme of parting: true closeness is an acceptance of distance, a nearness which is rediscovered at the furthest extent of separation.

Oh, not to be separate . . . Written in Paris, Summer 1925. A thin but powerful screen separates human inner space from the space of the world. True inwardness is not this walled-in ego, but an intensification of the outer world within our awareness, so that our inner space can host bird-flight and winds.

Reluctance to accept . . . Written in late October 1925 at Muzot. We place so much value on the future, on what's next, that we feel the need to ask its permission to enjoy the present moment. Absurdly, we even look forward to the next moment in order to look back on the present moment — a kind of anticipated nostalgia.

Do you really believe . . . Written around New Year 1926 at Val-Mont. The world is a seeing (not blind) world, as well as one that is seen by us. But we believe that we are the only perceiving subjects, *opposite* (facing, opposed to, separate from) a world of objects, which plop into our perceptions like billiard balls dropping into a pocket. This delightfully absurd image shows our naivete in thinking we can "pot" objects in this neat, decisive way.

How much obedience . . . Written on 10 March 1926 as a dedication in a volume of Rilke's translations of Paul Valéry's poetry given to Veronika Erdmann, a writer of Baltic origin. Rilke offers two alternative visions of the poetic process. Does it consist of yielding to the music of earth, channeling it obediently and passively into the poem? Or is it a matter of struggle, resistance and risk, with the poet as a murderer (albeit one without a knife), forcing experience into art by an act of daring violence? Perhaps these passive and aggressive modes are complementary: surrender and struggle are both aspects of the poetic vocation.

At long last . . . Written at Muzot in mid-June 1926, one of Rilke's last completed poems. The window is evoked both as a feature of daily domestic life, and as a symbol of transition or mediation between the inward and outward dimensions of human life. As a symbol, the Window (spoken of as a Platonic Form, of which particular earthly windows are only imitations) ranks with the Lyre and Swan, also important sacred images for Rilke, both being neighbouring constellations in the northern sky. The window gives each house an outlook, a view of distance beyond domestic confines. However bleak the view it holds, any window represents the possibility of transcendence. Yet its frame also represents limitation and loss as well as promise. The window is also a projection of Fate (Rilke's term for the limiting conditions of human life). It is at once constant (the structure) and changing (the contents of the view), offering both limited and unlimited visibility.

Rose, oh pure contradiction . . . Rilke's epitaph was composed at Muzot on 10 October 1925 as part of his will, and in accordance with his instructions it is inscribed on his grave in the churchyard of Raron in Switzerland. Shortly before, Rilke had written *Cimetière*, a prose poem in French, which asks how flowers (at a grave, for example) can escape from our human meanings and become *"rose-seule, rien-que-rose"* (only rose, nothing but rose). Then follows the mysterious phrase *"Sommeil de personne sous tant de paupières"* whose German equivalent ends the epitaph. The "pure contradiction" symbolized by the rose is perhaps between the intimately personal quality of our experience of Nature (the rose petals are as close as our eyelids) and the impersonal otherness of the rose in itself, which will always elude human appropriation. These experiences may also relieve us temporarily of the constrictions of our own personalities, so we become "no one," an empty receptacle for the world's plenitude.

ABOUT THE TRANSLATOR

—

Graham Good resides in Vancouver and teaches English and Comparative Literature at the University of British Columbia. He has wide interests, ranging from European literature to Buddhist philosophy, and has published books on contemporary literary theory — *Humanism Betrayed: Theory, Ideology and Culture in the Contemporary University* (Kingston and Montreal: McGill-Queen's University Press, 2001), and on the essay as a literary form — *The Observing Self: Rediscovering the Essay* (London and New York: Routledge, 1988). He has been involved in the "endless fascination" of translating Rilke's poetry since a version of *The Sonnets to Orpheus* formed part of his PhD in Comparative Literature at Princeton University. His verse translations of Rilke have grown over a long period of exploration, reflection and revision.